OPPOSING VIEWPOINTS®

Other Books of Related Interest

OPPOSING VIEWPOINTS®

American Values

Jennifer A. Hurley, *Book Editor*

David L. Bender, *Publisher*
Bruno Leone, *Executive Editor*
Bonnie Szumski, *Editorial Director*
David M. Haugen, *Managing Editor*

OPPOSING
VIEWPOINTS®
SERIES

Greenhaven Press, Inc., San Diego, California

Cover photo: PhotoDisc, Inc.

Library of Congress Cataloging-in-Publication Data

American values : opposing viewpoints / Jennifer A. Hurley, book
  editor.
      p.   cm. — (Opposing viewpoints series)
    Includes bibliographical references and index.
    ISBN 0-7377-0343-1 (pbk. : alk. paper). —
ISBN 0-7377-0344-X (lib. : alk. paper)
    1. United States—Moral conditions. 2. Social values.
I. Hurley, Jennifer A., 1973–   . II. Opposing viewpoints series
(Unnumbered)

HN90.M6 A45 2000
306'.0973—dc21   99-088159
                                                                        CIP

Greenhaven Press, Inc., P.O. Box 289009
San Diego, CA 92198-9009

"Congress shall make no law. . .abridging the freedom of speech, or of the press."

First Amendment to the U.S. Constitution

The basic foundation of our democracy is the First Amendment guarantee of freedom of expression. The Opposing Viewpoints Series is dedicated to the concept of this basic freedom and the idea that it is more important to practice it than to enshrine it.

Contents

Why Consider Opposing Viewpoints?

"The only way in which a human being can make some approach to knowing the whole of a subject is by hearing what can be said about it by persons of every variety of opinion and studying all modes in which it can be looked at by every character of mind. No wise man ever acquired his wisdom in any mode but this."

John Stuart Mill

In our media-intensive culture it is not difficult to find differing opinions. Thousands of newspapers and magazines and dozens of radio and television talk shows resound with differing points of view. The difficulty lies in deciding which opinion to agree with and which "experts" seem the most credible. The more inundated we become with differing opinions and claims, the more essential it is to hone critical reading and thinking skills to evaluate these ideas. Opposing Viewpoints books address this problem directly by presenting stimulating debates that can be used to enhance and teach these skills. The varied opinions contained in each book examine many different aspects of a single issue. While examining these conveniently edited opposing views, readers can develop critical thinking skills such as the ability to compare and contrast authors' credibility, facts, argumentation styles, use of persuasive techniques, and other stylistic tools. In short, the Opposing Viewpoints Series is an ideal way to attain the higher-level thinking and reading skills so essential in a culture of diverse and contradictory opinions.

In addition to providing a tool for critical thinking, Opposing Viewpoints books challenge readers to question their own strongly held opinions and assumptions. Most people form their opinions on the basis of upbringing, peer pressure, and personal, cultural, or professional bias. By reading carefully balanced opposing views, readers must directly confront new ideas as well as the opinions of those with whom they disagree. This is not to simplistically argue that everyone who reads opposing views will—or should—change his or her opinion. Instead, the series enhances readers' understanding of their own views by encouraging confrontation with opposing ideas. Careful examination of others' views can lead to the readers' understanding of the logical inconsistencies in their own opinions, perspective on why they hold an opinion, and the consideration of the possibility that their opinion requires further evaluation.

Evaluating Other Opinions

To ensure that this type of examination occurs, Opposing Viewpoints books present all types of opinions. Prominent spokespeople on different sides of each issue as well as well-known professionals from many disciplines challenge the reader. An additional goal of the series is to provide a forum for other, less known, or even unpopular viewpoints. The opinion of an ordinary person who has had to make the decision to cut off life support from a terminally ill relative, for example, may be just as valuable and provide just as much insight as a medical ethicist's professional opinion. The editors have two additional purposes in including these less known views. One, the editors encourage readers to respect others' opinions—even when not enhanced by professional credibility. It is only by reading or listening to and objectively evaluating others' ideas that one can determine whether they are worthy of consideration. Two, the inclusion of such viewpoints encourages the important critical thinking skill of objectively evaluating an author's credentials and bias. This evaluation will illuminate an author's reasons for taking a particular stance on an issue and will aid in readers' evaluation of the author's ideas.

As series editors of the Opposing Viewpoints Series, it is our hope that these books will give readers a deeper understanding of the issues debated and an appreciation of the complexity of even seemingly simple issues when good and honest people disagree. This awareness is particularly important in a democratic society such as ours in which people enter into public debate to determine the common good.

Those with whom one disagrees should not be regarded as enemies but rather as people whose views deserve careful examination and may shed light on one's own.

Thomas Jefferson once said that "difference of opinion leads to inquiry, and inquiry to truth." Jefferson, a broadly educated man, argued that "if a nation expects to be ignorant and free . . . it expects what never was and never will be." As individuals and as a nation, it is imperative that we consider the opinions of others and examine them with skill and discernment. The Opposing Viewpoints Series is intended to help readers achieve this goal.

David L. Bender & Bruno Leone,
Series Editors

Greenhaven Press anthologies primarily consist of previously published material taken from a variety of sources, including periodicals, books, scholarly journals, newspapers, government documents, and position papers from private and public organizations. These original sources are often edited for length and to ensure their accessibility for a young adult audience. The anthology editors also change the original titles of these works in order to clearly present the main thesis of each viewpoint and to explicitly indicate the opinion presented in the viewpoint. These alterations are made in consideration of both the reading and comprehension levels of a young adult audience. Every effort is made to ensure that Greenhaven Press accurately reflects the original intent of the authors included in this anthology.

Introduction

"Relativism must play a role in our analysis of moral and ethical issues. We don't live in a static world of absolutes."
—*John Hamerlinck*

"[Relativism] . . . sanctions obviously immoral actions, it implies that people are morally infallible, and it denies that there are any substantive moral disputes."
—*Theodore Schick Jr.*

In December of 1998, the House impeached President Bill Clinton on charges that he had lied under oath and obstructed justice in order to conceal his past sexual relationship with former White House intern Monica Lewinsky. From the time accusations were first made against Clinton in early 1998 until he was finally acquitted by the Senate in February 1999, the scandal drew a frenzy of media attention. News shows provided 24-hour coverage, *The Starr Report* disclosed intimate details about the affair, and Lewinsky's photograph was a ubiquitous sight.

Opinion polls offer an intriguing glimpse at the public's reaction to Clinton's behavior. Most Americans—70 percent as of August 1998—felt that the president lacked high ethical or moral standards. However, a December 1998 Gallup poll conducted during the impeachment proceedings found that Clinton's approval rating was at 73 percent, the highest of his presidency. According to a *Washington Post* poll, half of Americans agreed that as long as the president does a good job, "whatever he does in his personal life is not important."

Some analysts say that the public's reluctance to judge Clinton's behavior is symptomatic of society's moral relativism—the belief that morality is a matter of individual choice. John F. Kavanaugh, who teaches ethics and religion at St. Louis University, summarizes moral relativism as the attitude that "Who can be so arrogant as to tell others that they are right or wrong?"

Critics assert that the philosophy of moral relativism, because it refuses to support definite moral rules, makes it difficult for people to condemn any behavior, no matter how evil. Philosophy professor Francis Beckwith writes that "If . . . moral and religious life is only a matter of personal tastes, preferences, and orientations . . . , then we cannot tell young people it's wrong to lie, steal, cheat, abuse drugs, or kill their newborns."

Furthermore, claim Beckwith and others, moral relativism depends on the belief that God does not exist. As writer Cheryl Borrowdale explains, "Most major world religions, including Christianity, Judaism, and Islam, traditionally rely on the supposition that God exists and has set forth moral rules. If, however, God has set forth moral rules, then morality cannot be relative." According to critics of moral relativism, the laws set down by God provide a code of morality that is absolute and unwavering.

Writer John Hamerlinck contends that relativists are not atheists, but simply believe that moral issues have few absolutes. He offers one scenario as evidence that morality depends upon circumstances: Suppose a murderer were stalking your friend—should you lie to the murderer about your friend's whereabouts? Hamerlinck asks: "How many people, Christian or otherwise, would not lie in that situation? Is lying therefore an absolute moral wrong? No, because ethics are inescapably situational. Although there is general agreement across the ideological spectrum that lying is wrong, there are still situations in which it is the morally correct thing to do."

The contrasting philosophies of morality posed by scholars such as Beckwith and Hamerlinck play a role in a wide spectrum of issues. For example, on the issue of sexuality, moral absolutists argue that homosexuality, premarital sex, and adultery are always wrong, since they are prohibited by the Bible, while moral relativists believe that sexuality is a question of personal choice and that individuals are accountable to their own consciences. While individuals ultimately decide what ethical system, if any, they choose to follow, society plays a strong role in determining which values are upheld and which are discouraged. The authors of

American Values: Opposing Viewpoints, in the chapters What Values Should America Uphold? Is America in Moral Decline? How Do the Media Influence American Values? and What Measures Would Improve American Values?, provide a variety of perspectives on the state of moral values in American society.

CHAPTER 1

What Values Should America Uphold?

Chapter Preface

At a rally at the end of May 1999, Democratic presidential candidate Al Gore, denouncing the "hollow secularism" of American society, called for religion to play a greater role in addressing the needs of the public. Both Gore and Republican presidential candidate George W. Bush support a program called Charitable Choice, which would allocate federal funds to religious institutions that provide social services for the homeless, mentally ill, and those addicted to drugs.

The philosophy behind Charitable Choice is that religious institutions are inherently more effective than government bureaucracies in helping disadvantaged members of society. As columnist William Raspberry explains, "Church ministries have rescued drug addicts and alcoholics who formerly were in and out of all sorts of public and private clinics. . . . These groups have been successful because they don't simply deliver treatment and other services; they transform." Because churches provide spiritual counseling as well as practical aid, say advocates of Charitable Choice, they make a lasting impact on participants' lives in a way that government programs cannot.

While supporters view the program as an innovative and promising approach to curing social ills, others regard Charitable Choice as a grievous threat to Americans' freedom of religion. If Charitable Choice goes into effect, charge critics, people in need of public assistance may be forced to adopt particular religious beliefs in order to receive help. Furthermore, critics claim that Charitable Choice would compromise the integrity of churches themselves. In the view of commentator Melissa Rogers, "Instead of being known as sanctuaries, churches could come to be viewed essentially as arms of the state. If tax subsidies flow to churches and other religious ministries, the role of religion as prophetic critic of government . . . will be diminished."

The debate over government financing of church ministries highlights the question of what role religion should play in the public sphere. The following chapter offers disparate views on religion and other forces that shape morality in America.

"Capitalism . . . is rooted in a belief in the ultimate worth of the individual."

Capitalism Promotes Positive Values

Theodore Forstmann

In the viewpoint that follows, Theodore Forstmann argues that free-market capitalism is essential to a democratic society. By ensuring a free, stable environment, contends Forstmann, capitalism affirms the autonomy of the individual and prevents the government from gaining too much power. Forstmann is the founding general partner of the New York investment firm Forstmann Little & Co., and the founding chairman of Empower America, an organization that supports free-market principles.

As you read, consider the following questions:

1. As explained by Forstmann, what did America's Founding Fathers believe was the appropriate role of government?
2. What is the central promise of capitalism, as stated by Forstmann?
3. According to the author, how does capitalism make a democratic society possible?

Excerpted from "Capitalism and Democracy American-Style: Can They Co-exist?" by Theodore Forstmann, at www.empower.org/html/pubs/speeches/capdem.htm. Reprinted with permission.

Editor's note: The following viewpoint was excerpted from a speech delivered to Grant's Political Conference in New York City on June 8, 1994.

America, unique in all the world, began with the idea of government as the quiet guardian of freedom, the old idea of the "night watchman state." This vision of our country remained largely intact until the Great Depression. Unnerved by that horrible event, the thought that government could do a whole variety of things that the individual could not, became embedded in the public psyche. Subsequently, in ever increasing increments, we have accepted the idea that government can be a substitute for freedom, and public compassion can replace personal virtue.

And really, we have no excuse for abandoning our principles. Throughout our history, America's great leaders have reminded us often of just that danger. All, until recent times, spoke of "human liberty" and "limited government" almost interchangeably. If Thomas Jefferson were attending this conference, he would probably remind us of his own simple formulation about political and economic power. "That government is best," he said, "which governs least." Or he might recycle his famous line that "government can do something for the people only in proportion as it can do something to the people." Thirteen presidents later, the same principle was still taken as a given. "I go for a government," said Lincoln, "doing for the people that which they cannot do better for themselves." Even Woodrow Wilson, were he here today, could remind us of his own warning in 1912 that "the history of liberty is the history of the limitation of government, not its expansion."

No political freedom, their words echo down to us, is secure where the right to property, the fruit of one's own intellectual or physical labor, is not strong. Government's job, our Founders all believed, was basically to create a stable environment in which free people could operate; to provide the permanent political conditions in which economic changes would inevitably occur. This was all basic noncontroversial stuff. And so, for example, in Wilson's day, Americans paid no more than 10 percent of their earnings to all levels of government. When the income tax was first proposed in 1909, one senator rose to suggest a constitutional limit of ten percent. And it's staggering to reflect how this suggestion was greeted. After further heated debate, the idea was rejected on the grounds that if a ten percent maximum were set, the income tax might inevitably rise to that ominous level.

The Apologetic Capitalist

Take all the endless warnings of our past leaders against unchecked political power, and what we have is the enduring moral case for the free market. But we forgot those warnings. Along came a class of people telling us that capitalism is a crass, selfish, depressing vision of human possibilities, that under their guidance we could do better. And, to a large extent, we bought it. We believed them, to the point that even today we take the expanded powers of government as a given, something scarcely worth questioning. To me, few figures today are more pathetic than the apologetic capitalist. He has surrendered to the idea that making money is the only goal; that the essence of economic activity is subsidies and penalties; that collectivism and entitlement, and the corresponding lack of opportunity, are alright—just so long as he gets his piece. He is like a holdup victim pleading to keep his empty wallet, who doesn't even question anymore whether government is acting within its proper bounds. A subsidy here, a tax break there, and soon fundamental principles are right out the window. He ends up articulating the problem in government's own debasing terminology of "who gets what" from its distributive powers. The elites have set up a giant bustling industry with millions of bureaucratic dependents and little by little, they buy us off with scraps of state power. They set their own boundaries, closer and closer to our lives and indeed closer and closer to our souls.

Even politicians who claim to represent democratic capitalism only argue on the margins, while the central principles are quietly abandoned. In both parties, we find ourselves locked in ferocious debate over the details of state expansion—the timing, method and funding schedule of our own national and moral decline. I strongly believe that most

Americans would survey the fruits of the modern welfare state and conclude that the experiment has been a failure. Really it's a scene of human wreckage that brings to my mind the old lines from Samuel Johnson:

> How small, of all that human hearts endure, that part which laws or kings can cause or cure.

The tragedy is that American capitalism arose precisely to prevent this state of affairs. The relationship between capitalism and American democracy always depended upon the simple enough insight that neither could succeed without the other, that both worked to the same end. That end was not just wealth creation. It was human liberty. Capitalism did not promise a world of perfect security. Perfect security under the state was precisely the thing America renounced at its founding. It did not, unlike the socialist world we have seen collapsing all around us, promise a blueprint for blissful equality and freedom from failure. It promised only freedom, with all the risks that entails, all the endless possibilities for success or failure.

Capitalism and Democracy

Indeed, for all its rough edges, one cannot pay the free market a great enough tribute. It is hardly a system to be apologetic about. We think of capitalism as an outgrowth of democracy. But historically it happened the other way around. Modern democracy came into the world through capitalism at the close of the Middle Ages. It came into being because it ultimately afforded the only escape from the tyranny of religious theories and men who benefited from them. Capitalism is not a materialist vision. It is rooted in a belief in the ultimate worth of the individual. And, although supremely practical, it functions well fundamentally because of giving—not taking; of investing and producing—not consuming and destroying. Unlike modern government, it does not try to palm itself off as the answer to all human problems. It simply acknowledges that God made our individual lives to be meaningful enough without us all being herded into vast collective endeavors—with perfect happiness and security just beyond the next New Deal, Five Year Plan, or Great Leap Forward. It declares that our lives are our own

19

to live; our decisions, within reasonable bounds, our own to make; our property fundamentally our own to use as we think best.

Is this a crass, selfish vision of life? Not to me. To me, it has always seemed a profoundly optimistic vision. Where socialist schemes arise from a deep wariness of people, capitalism regards the ordinary person as a moral actor, flawed yet competent to work out his or her own fate. It may not be perfect, but the free market is so far the world's only workable vision of men without masters. It understands that life's great dramas are private ones, that goodness and compassion work better as personal virtues than federal mandates. It is a system based on trust of the ordinary person. It is not a license for rapacity—it's a pact of self-discipline, above all on the part of government.

The Promises of Capitalism

Democratic capitalism has not built a "New Jerusalem," nor has it returned us to the "law of the jungle." It promises, instead, three extraordinary things: liberation from abject poverty, freedom from political tyranny, and release of the individual conscience from oppression.

No human system has ever kept its promises more faithfully. Democratic capitalism has been history's best weapon against poverty, oppression, and tyranny. Free markets have generated unequaled living standards for unrivaled numbers of men and women. Yet capitalism's accomplishments are much deeper. Its enduring appeal is not its toasters, televisions, and transistors, but its respect for individual innovation, creativity, and upward mobility.

Capitalism has never been a utopian vision, unlike socialism. It never promised to build the Kingdom of God on earth. But it has succeeded in allowing people to stand upright and dignified in the kingdoms of this world. . . .

Consider the virtues of capitalism. An ethic of work, savings, and self-reliance. The integrity and honesty essential to contracts, trade, and money. A passion for excellence. The impulse given to charity and philanthropy. All these things depend on values, not on greed. A free market does not insist on perfect virtue, but it does depend on common morality.

Jack Kemp, speech delivered at a conference entitled *Culture Wars: The Battle over Family Values*, February 22, 1994.

If our faith in the individual created and built America; if even now polling data demonstrates that 70% of Americans are disillusioned with government and believe that "when something is run by government it is usually inefficient and wasteful"; if our free market economy is now the model and inspiration for countries around the world—why, as these countries make their way towards democratic capitalism, do they find us straggling in the other direction?

The Greed of Big Government

Well, let's see if there is a perfectly rational answer. Again and again, one has the surreal experience of hearing those in power speaking as if it were all a grand success—all the lawyers and activists and professional staffers and academics who make up the state and the multiple members of the media who make their livelihood writing and talking about it. Only after a while does it dawn on you that, from the standpoint of all these people, big government, the statist model, is a great and historic success simply because they personally benefit from it. . . .

Nowhere in all of modern America can one see greater greed for power than amongst these people themselves. Actually, the grasping greedy taxer of today is far more destructive and devouring than the worst imaginable excess any free market could possibly produce. Unfortunately, these people are not overburdened with either modesty or practicality. At the Kennedy School [of Government] and similar places—they learn all the arcana of government, the flow charts, percentiles, depreciation schedules and theories of redistribution.

But our ruling elite do not, by and large, come to public office via the productive private endeavors they aspire to rule and reshape. They learn to do the only thing government can do: to gather and dispose of the fruits of other people's enterprise. What they don't learn is how to earn, create, or produce. Perhaps no one has described this mentality better than Winston Churchill. Big government, he said, "is the philosophy of failure, the creed of ignorance, and the gospel of envy."

Unfortunately, we are governed by people who do not agree with Churchill's sentiments. They are people unacquainted with the nobility of private life to whom we are only ciphers to be formed into aggregates. It's really that simple.

Less simple is the fact that Americans themselves have consented to this self-abandonment. We are less free by choice. We can speak of our "estrangement" from government, of how the system is failing us. We can say people are being "bought off" by politicians, seduced, misled, betrayed—whatever. But aren't these all symptoms of the illness rather than the cause? Isn't the fundamental question this: Have we lost confidence in our worth as individuals?

In reality, despite the tired and overused excuse of the complexity of the times we live in, we face the same simple, hard questions free people have always faced: real risk or false security, individual worth or collectivism, opportunity or entitlement. I would like more than anything to end with a resounding assurance that we will make the right choice; a statement that surely, being Americans, of course, we believe in ourselves, and of course in the end we will find the way back. Unfortunately, the evidence is too ambiguous. I can only hope that Thomas Paine was wrong in fearing that one day, "A thousand years hence, perhaps in less, America may be what Europe is now . . . the noblest work of human wisdom, the grand scene of human glory, the fair cause of freedom that rose and fell."

"Against the moral basis of virtually every world religion, selfishness [is] the goal [of a capitalist society]."

Capitalism Does Not Promote Positive Values

David Hilfiker

David Hilfiker asserts in the following viewpoint that capitalism, the "new religion" of American society, promotes values that are morally questionable. He argues that capitalism celebrates a philosophy of self-interest, undermines the dignity of work, and uses money as the measuring stick for everything—including people. Hilfiker is a physician who works with the inner-city poor.

As you read, consider the following questions:
1. In Hilfiker's view, what five assumptions of capitalism have shaped American assumptions about life?
2. How has the capitalist focus on profit impacted society's values, in the author's opinion?
3. According to Hilfiker, how is the free-market system unjust?

Excerpted from "Naming Our Gods," by David Hilfiker, *The Other Side*, July/August 1998. Reprinted with the permission of *The Other Side*.

For fifteen years, I've worked as a physician with the inner-city poor as part of a small Christian community. Our work is grounded in the understanding that God calls us to care for and move into solidarity with those who have been—for whatever reason—excluded from society.

Several times a month, I travel to talk about our work—mostly to medical students or groups. Their questions have become predictable and troubling. Increasingly I feel like a visitor from another time.

"Dr. Hilfiker, what do your wife and children think about your living in the city and working with very poor people?" The underlying assumption seems to be that I must have dragged my family kicking and screaming into the urban jungle. (If anyone did the dragging, it was my wife Marja, and our children's lives have been greatly enriched.)

"Dr. Hilfiker, you're obviously an extraordinary person. [They really say that!] You've been able to give up a doctor's salary to work with the poor. But you certainly can't expect most young doctors to be able to do what you've done."

This perception of my extraordinary sacrifice persists even though I've mentioned in my talk that Marja's and my combined income (around $45,000) puts us *well above* the median income in this country, and I've made clear that we reap the benefits of community and meaningful vocations in ways most people only dream of. Try as I might, I cannot seem to undermine the perception of our sainthood.

"Dr. Hilfiker, I really want to do work like yours. That's why I came to medical school. But now I'm not sure I could give up all the other stuff. I've really become attached to our lifestyle. And I see the older students starting to believe they deserve those enormous salaries. I'm not sure I can hold out! Besides, with the debts I'm racking up, I don't know how to do anything like what you've done. I feel like I'm getting lost."

Forty years ago, doctors assumed they had a responsibility to serve poor people. For the most part, they accepted that responsibility gratefully. Many thousands of doctors did work similar to mine, and no one thought to remark much upon it. But today, doctors (or, for that matter, any affluent people) who voluntarily move into solidarity with the poor are considered "saints," while those who sacrifice perhaps more for careers in politics, the arts, or business are considered "normal."

The Religion of Capitalism

Some fundamental set of societal values has shifted, co-opting the ways in which we think. Today, we have trouble understanding service, sharing, justice, and equality, not because we are worse people than forty years ago, but because, over the last generation, we've unwittingly transformed capitalism into a religion. . . .

The assumptions underlying capitalism have become essential metaphors in our deepest thinking about our society and ourselves. Unawares, we've allowed the language of capitalism to shape our basic assumptions about our lives—not only economic, but also social, political, and spiritual.

An older edition of the basic college textbook *Economics*, authored by Paul Samuelson, names the five underlying assumptions of capitalism.

① Five Underlying Assumptions of Capitalism

First, capitalism assumes the economic system works best if each person pursues his or her selfish good, that is, the greatest profit. In *The Wealth of Nations*, Adam Smith proclaimed the principle of the 'invisible hand': "Every individual, in pursuing only his own selfish good, [is] led as if by an invisible hand, to achieve the best good for all . . ."

Second, the profit motive drives economics. The *only* basis for making economic decisions is what brings the greatest profit.

Third, in order to make economic decisions, everything must have a price, including human labor. "Money . . . provides the measuring rod of values."

Fourth, decisions about whom to produce things for are determined by supply and demand, by relative income. The distribution of goods and services, therefore, is determined by the distribution of private wealth.

Fifth, wealth is primarily private property. "'Capitalism' got its name because . . . capital or 'wealth' is primarily the private property of somebody—the capitalist." The output of a business (after market-determined wages are paid) belongs to the "owner" of the capital.

These assumptions may or may not be the best ones upon which to build an economic system. In fact, most modern economists recognize their weaknesses, and most Western economies are significantly modified forms of capitalism. I'd like to explore how these assumptions have invaded our basic ideological and spiritual framework, affecting us to the point where they have become our new religion.

The "Invisible Hand"

It is worth, then, revisiting the principles laid out in the Samuelson text with a critical, contemporary eye. How might they have affected our spirits? How might we root ourselves again in biblical perspectives?

Take the first—Adam Smith's "invisible hand." In effect, Smith said that if we were steadfastly selfish in our economic decisions, the "invisible hand" would make of everyone's selfish decisions a tapestry that benefits us all. We have not only the permission but also the responsibility to look only after our own self-interest.

This is a breathtaking supposition! Against the moral basis of virtually every world religion, selfishness becomes the goal. To be sure, it's been conclusively demonstrated that this assumption has overwhelming power to increase economic production. But do we want to enshrine selfishness as a primary value by which we *live*?

But we have. Self-interest has become so basic that we can hardly think outside it.

And yet, in the not-so-distant past, we were able to consider many other factors—and did. For example, Marja was born and reared in Finland. When she and I fell in love, her father argued strongly against her relocation to the United States. Finland was a small country, he said, and had invested in her by providing her free education through college. Now she was a teacher and a valuable national resource. She had a responsibility to her society to stay in Finland.

To the modern ear, this argument seemed quaint—almost humorous. Our first inclination was to see in it *his* self-interest. But it was a straightforward argument he deeply believed: One has a responsibility to one's society that can override one's self-interest.

Today, pop psychology counsels us that self-interest is the necessary ground of good relationships. Only by "looking after number one," it argues, can we relate mutually to each other. I sometimes catch myself defending my work with poor people by pointing out how much I get out of it. That's true, of course, but why do I need to claim self-interest? Why is *love* or *justice* not an adequate excuse?

Yet how many of us really believe that selfishness is a virtue, or that the world really works better if we look only to our own best interest?

While Adam Smith's pursuit of self-interest may or may not make good economics, it shares no common ground with biblical ethics, which emphasize love, community, and justice for the poor.

The Profit Motive

What of the second assumption, that within the capitalist system the purpose of economic activity is profit? Monetary return becomes the guiding motive for economic activity: how much advertising to buy, how many widgets to make, whether to open a branch in Peoria, or whether to downsize a corporation.

But note how *profit* is defined. It does not include the wages of workers, from entry level positions to managers. Wages are paid before profit is calculated. The guiding principle for all economic activity, then, is to maximize returns for the "investors" (those who are wealthy enough to have assets to invest). Note that only those who put money into the system are considered investors; workers do not usually "invest" by working.

The difference between investing and gambling (that is, trying to get immense returns for minimal money) is not always clear, at least in the modern stock market. Gambling, of course, did not originate in capitalism; nor did Adam Smith encourage people to profit unfairly. But the concepts of capitalism have given a certain unconscious legitimacy to these attempts at easy money.

There is a powerful perception today that "getting something for nothing" is really the way the world works. What one receives has little to do with the sweat equity one puts in but rather with wealth and the right kind of "luck." This has seeped into every area of our society.

Undermining the Value of Work

Some workers have always received more than others for an hour of work time. To question this is a societal taboo. But in recent decades, the discrepancies have multiplied. Top athletes, entertainment stars, and CEOs are obvious examples. Yet in many instances, doctors, lawyers, accountants, and other professionals receive much more than can be attributed to their "work." Bill Gates's amassing a fortune of well over $10 billion in twenty-five years is seen as a positive example of American ingenuity and success rather than a warning of a horribly warped system.

This focus on profit, on earning money, has mushroomed beyond the sphere of economics to become central to our understanding of life itself. The purpose of work is to make money.

Capitalism's Dehumanization of Work

Karl Marx's severest moral indictment of capitalism was the alienation of labor. What he had in mind primarily was that the methods of production under capitalism, including the division of labor, in effect divorce workers from the products of their labor, for they do not express themselves in or realize any self-fulfillment in the products. They work only for external benefits. This is the prostitution of work. As in the case of the prostitution of sex, it robs work, one of the primary wells of meaning in human life, of its meaning. We should be as morally indignant about the prostitution of work as we are about the prostitution of sex, for meaningless work, like meaningless sex, is dehumanizing. It is a major factor in the demise of meaning in the modern age.

E.M. Adams, *Vital Speeches of the Day*, May 1, 1999.

Activities that are not financially remunerative, even those essential to societal well-being, are not valued. Is teaching the next generation less important than curing their physical ills? In our society, high salaries indicate that the work of a physician has more prestige and value than that of an elementary-school teacher. In Finland, on the other hand, the two earn approximately the same and carry equal status. In our society, the care of children at home—probably the most important thing we do for our future as a society—has no monetary value and is hardly considered a productive way to spend one's life.

The biblical view, of course, is that money is only a minor part of the purpose of work. We work to provide for the basic needs of our families and ourselves. But we also work out of love for others, to express our creativity, to be fulfilled, to create a better environment for our community, and to make a more just world. (Many people are reduced to working for money in an economic system that offers them nothing more, but that is clearly a violation of the biblical order.)

Why do students admire me for taking a salary 50 percent higher than the average salary in this country? I choose to do wonderfully meaningful, desperately needed, community-oriented work with profound intrinsic rewards—yet I become saintly because I decline work that would pay me more money than anyone really needs. A bizarre ideology captivates us!

The Bible judges the acquisition of surplus wealth to be inordinately dangerous to one's soul. Jesus was explicit about the pitfalls of wealth. Yet within capitalism, the primary purpose of the individual is the acquisition of surplus wealth. The societal desperation resulting from hoarded wealth is everywhere obvious. Yet our society (including the church) continues to exalt the accumulation of vast wealth.

What began as an innocuous economic principle has quietly seeped into our consciousness to reshape our underlying assumptions about the purpose of work, the goal of creativity, and the nature of humanity. That people within a capitalist system are oriented toward money is not a coincidence—it is a fundamental.

Everything Must Have a Price

The third assumption argues that everything must have a price, and that money is the measuring rod of value.

The mechanism used to allocate resources in the free-enterprise system is price. The question, in deciding whether to buy a new machine or hire new workers, is, "Which costs less?" To determine how much people value something, the statistician asks how much they would pay. In my own profession, medicine, cost-benefit economic analysis has become a primary way to choose among treatment options—even though it requires giving a dollar value to human life.

When the assumption that everything has a price filters into our value system, we find we must struggle to hang onto values that have no price tag. Building community (to say nothing of building the reign of God) has no dollar value, so the medical students I talk to have no foundation for thinking about a career working with the poor.

In such a system, the only way to mobilize social forces against poverty is to show how much money society would save by investing in poor neighborhoods, alternatives to prison, and preventative medical care. In other words, by a cost-benefit analysis of poverty.

Again, few of us *believe* that everything has a price tag. We know there is no way to calculate the value of having a family or doing meaningful work. Yet if we act on that obvious reality, we are considered hopeless idealists.

Of course, it is easy to pontificate against modern excesses around money. Consumerism, materialism, and purchased political patronage are easy targets. But most of us are not exempt from fawning upon the wealthy. The boards of our churches and nonprofits are filled with wealthy people who can raise money. Compare the number of teachers, nurses, and police officers to the numbers of lawyers and doctors who sit on those boards.

Even among devout Christians, "planning for one's future" means having enough money to take care of any future contingency. Why does planning for one's future *not* mean creating a strong community, or fostering deep love within one's children, or working for social change? Why is the hoarding of financial resources the only thing that builds future security?

The Injustice of Capitalism

Samuelson's fourth assumption states that the distribution of goods and services is determined by the distribution of private wealth. Those who have more money get more things.

This assumption is so deeply embedded in our value system that it's hard to even argue. If I ask, for instance, why, when compared with suburban schools, schools in poor areas are in physical disrepair, poorly supplied and equipped, and have low compensation for their teachers, the response is, "Well, the people in the city can't afford anything better."

Or if I ask, "Why do the children come to school hungry?" I hear back, "Well, their parents can't afford to give them anything for breakfast." Even if we don't like the responses, most of us will nod our head as if we had been given an "answer." But we haven't. We've only been given a statement of values.

③ An essential principle of the free-market system, then, is actually a formulation of injustice. The rich get whatever they want; the poor get nothing.

Again, few of us really believe that the world should operate this way. Some of us might agree to distribute *luxuries* according to wealth, but does anyone believe that food, shelter, basic education, healthcare, or other necessities should be distributed according to private wealth? Nonetheless, we have established a society in which even those necessities are meted out mostly on the basis of how much money people have.

It is important to understand that we have *chosen* this. Neither modern capitalism nor economic imperative requires that necessities be distributed according to wealth. Today's "capitalistic" economic systems can easily be modified through taxation and wealth-transfer programs, such as Social Security, to provide necessities for all.

Yet belief in the *religion* of capitalism is so deeply embedded in us that we have even, in the last few years, taken steps to dismantle the few societal mechanisms for providing necessities to those who—for one reason or another—do not possess private wealth. There seems to be an almost religious zeal for ensuring that nothing is left to the sentimentality of those who would make the basic societal needs available to all.

We have, in practice, accepted the basic injustice of the world as at least inevitable, if not proper. We seem incapable of the outrage of the prophets. We have lost our capacity for protest, our capacity to see and hold up alternatives.

The Sacredness of Private Property

This brings us to Samuelson's fifth and final assumption: Wealth is primarily private property that the owner can dispose of as he or she wishes.

Nothing is more deeply established in our economic system, more enshrined in popular consciousness, than the sacredness of "private property." Capitalism, of course, is dependent on the notion that the wealth a person amasses belongs to him or her. Without "private property," one could not have a capitalist system, since people cannot invest what they do not own.

Yet this value has gone far deeper than our ownership of things. To take my profession, physicians no longer feel much responsibility to society, even though society invests heavily in the education of physicians. (The cost to society to educate one doctor is over $1 million.) Instead, they view their degrees as "theirs" and believe they are free to use them as they will.

The assumption of "private property," nestled into our very being, has eroded our consciousness of the ties that link us to family, community, nation, and world. *My* things, *my* education, *my* abilities, *my* ideas—they all belong to me. My possessions and I become an island, separated from everyone else's islands.

It is common to hear that older people or younger couples without children have joined forces to vote down taxes for education in their community. The money belongs to them, and they have the legal right to vote against educating the future generations. But do we want to grant anyone the moral right to secede from the community?

The Native American concept that no one owns the land is well known. That most of us have difficulty even imagining life under such a concept—despite the obvious ravages to the environment under private ownership—is a sign of how deeply we have accepted the notion of "private property."

Here in Washington's inner city, I know capable, desperately poor people who remain poor essentially because they are always helping their less able relatives out of financial crises. If they saved money, I suspect, they would be able to leave their decaying neighborhood, but each payday they feel bound to respond to the needs of relatives.

Most of us, finding ourselves in the same position, would question such behavior. Will our relatives use the money responsibly? Will the money ever get paid back? Aren't we just "enabling" the relatives to remain irresponsible? Couldn't we do more by moving to a better neighborhood and finding a way to bring the relatives along?

All such questions assume that the money we earn is *ours*. My inner-city friends apparently don't share the same assumption. Family has some claim on what they earn. For most of us, this is a concept beyond our imagining.

What the Bible Says

There is, of course, a different set of values, one that corresponds more closely to what, deep in our hearts, most of us feel is right and just. This is a set of values consistent with the gospel of Christ.

They might be as boldly and simply stated as Samuelson's points:

All men and women are our neighbors, and self-interest is not primary. "Love your neighbors as yourselves" (Matt. 22:39).

Our decisions shall be based on our love for God and God's creation. Profit is not the sole determinant. "What will a person profit by winning the whole world at the cost of one's true self?" (Matt. 16:25).

The value of a person, a product, or a part of nature is determined by its intrinsic value, not by how much people will pay for it. "Not one of the sparrows, which sell two for five pence, is overlooked by God. Have no fear, you are worth more than any number of sparrows" (Luke 12:6-8).

Necessities for everyone come before luxuries for some. Until all have obtained necessities, decisions about what is produced should not be based on who has the most money. "Those who had much didn't have too much; those who had little had enough" (II Cor. 8:15).

The bounty of the earth is not private property but a gift

from God that belongs to God. "The earth is God's, and all the fullness thereof" (Psalm 24:1).

Western society hungers for values deeper than those it has. Even people who do not call themselves spiritual sense that something is desperately askew.

At a moral level, they realize that it isn't right for homeless families to walk the streets of the richest nation on earth. They know that global warming is dangerous and destructive. They acknowledge that people have a responsibility to one another. . . .

The function of religion in the human community should be to call forth our best and highest selves. As an economic system, capitalism may or may not serve us well. As a religion, especially an unnamed one, it is disastrous.

We must recognize where we are. We must find in our spirits the willingness to follow another way. We must share what we have found.

"Unless modern thinkers can locate a source of moral authority . . . , we will always be vulnerable to the dangerous swings of moral consensus."

Religion Is Essential to a Moral Society

Philip Yancey

Philip Yancey explains in the subsequent viewpoint why a moral society is necessarily a religious society. He claims that contemporary America's secularism has reduced the concept of morality to a question of personal choice. According to Yancey, the ability to make authentic judgments about right and wrong requires the guidance of religion; any moral system set down by secularists is completely arbitrary, since it has no higher authority as its foundation. Yancey is the author of many books, including the recent *What's So Amazing About Grace?*

As you read, consider the following questions:
1. How has the concept of morality changed in recent years, according to Yancey?
2. What does Yancey charge is the fate of a society that has lost moral consensus?
3. Why, in the author's view, is it impossible for secularists to defend any system of morality?

Excerpted from "Nietzsche Was Right," by Philip Yancey, *Books & Culture*, January/February 1998. Reprinted with permission from the author.

A representative of Generation X named Sam told me he had been discovering the strategic advantages of truth. As an experiment, he decided to stop lying. "It helps people picture you and relate to you more reliably," he said. "Truth can be positively beneficial in many ways."

I asked what would happen if he found himself in a situation where it would prove *more* beneficial for him to lie. He said he would have to judge the context, but he was trying to prefer not-lying.

For Sam, the decision to lie or tell the truth involved not morality but a social construct, to be adopted or rejected as a matter of expedience. In essence, the source of moral authority for Sam is himself, and that in a nutshell is the dilemma confronting moral philosophy in the postmodern world.

The Rise of Unmorality

Something unprecedented in human history is brewing: a rejection of external moral sources altogether. Individuals and societies have always been immoral to varying degrees. Individuals (never an entire society) have sometimes declared themselves amoral, professing agnosticism about ethical matters. Only recently, however, have serious thinkers entertained the notion of unmorality: that there is no such thing as morality. A trend prefigured by Nietzsche, prophesied by Dostoyevsky, and analyzed presciently by C.S. Lewis in *The Abolition of Man* is now coming to fruition. The very concept of morality is undergoing a profound change, led in part by the advance guard of a new science called "evolutionary psychology."

So far, however, the pioneers of unmorality have practiced a blatant contradiction. Following in the style of Jean-Paul Sartre, who declared that meaningful communication is impossible even as he devoted his life to communicating meaningfully, the new moralists first proclaim that morality is capricious, perhaps even a joke, then proceed to use moral categories to condemn their opponents. These new high priests lecture us solemnly about multiculturalism, gender equality, homophobia, and environmental degradation, all the while ignoring the fact that they have systematically destroyed any basis for judging such behavior right or wrong. The emperor so quick to discourse about fashion happens to be stark naked. . . .

In a great irony, the "politically correct" movement defending the rights of women, minorities, and the environment often positions itself as an enemy of the Christian church when, in historical fact, the church has contributed the very underpinnings that make such a movement possible. Christianity brought an end to slavery, and its crusading fervor also fueled the early labor movement, women's suffrage, human-rights campaigns, and civil rights. According to Robert Bellah, "there has not been a major issue in the history of the United States on which religious bodies did not speak out, publicly and vociferously."

It was no accident that Christians pioneered in the antislavery movement, for their beliefs had a theological impetus. Both slavery and the oppression of women were based, anachronistically, on an embryonic form of Darwinism. Aristotle had observed that

> Tame animals are naturally better than wild animals, yet for all tame animals there is an advantage in being under human control, as this secures their survival. And as regards the relationship between male and female, the former is naturally superior, the latter inferior, the former rules and the latter is subject. By analogy, the same must necessarily apply to mankind as a whole. Therefore all men who differ from one another by as much as the soul differs from the body or man from a wild beast (and that is the state of those who work by using their bodies, and for whom that is the best they can do)—these people are slaves by nature, and it is better for them to be subject to this kind of control, as it is better for the other creatures I have mentioned. . . . It is clear that there are certain people who are free and certain people who are slaves by nature, and it is both to their advantage, and just, for them to be slaves. . . . From the hour of their birth, some men are marked out for subjection, others for rule.

Cross out the name *Aristotle* and read the paragraph again as the discovery of a leading evolutionary psychologist. No one is proposing the reimposition of slavery, of course—but why not? If we learn our morality from nature, and if our only rights are those we create for ourselves, why should not the strong exercise their "natural rights" over the weak?

The Need for a Moral Authority

As Alasdair MacIntyre remarks in *After Virtue*, modern protesters have not abandoned moral argument, though they have abandoned any coherent platform from which to make a moral argument. They keep using moral terminology—it is *wrong* to own slaves, rape a woman, abuse a child, despoil the environment, discriminate against homosexuals—but they have no "higher authority" to which to appeal to make their moral judgments. MacIntyre concludes,

> Hence the *utterance* of protest is characteristically addressed to those who already *share* the protestors' premises. The effects of incommensurability ensure that protestors rarely have anyone else to talk to but themselves. This is not to say that protest cannot be effective; it is to say that it cannot be *rationally* effective and that its dominant modes of expression give evidence of a certain perhaps unconscious awareness of this.

In the United States, we prefer to settle major issues on utilitarian or pragmatic grounds. But philosophers including Aristotle and David Hume argued powerfully in favor of slavery on those very grounds. Hitler pursued his genocidal policies against the Jews and "defective" persons on utilitarian grounds. Unless modern thinkers can locate a source of moral authority somewhere else than in the collective sentiments of human beings, we will always be vulnerable to dangerous swings of moral consensus. . . .

A Generation of Wingless Chickens

It is easy to see that the moral sense has been bred out of certain sections of the population, like the wings have been bred off certain chickens to produce more white meat on them. This is a generation of wingless chickens.

—Flannery O'Connor

What happens when an entire society becomes populated with wingless chickens? I need not dwell on the contemporary symptoms of moral illness in the United States: our rate of violent crime has quintupled in my lifetime; a third of all babies are now born out of wedlock; half of all marriages end in divorce; the richest nation on earth has a homeless population larger than the entire population of some nations. These familiar symptoms are just that, symptoms. A diagnosis would look beyond them to our loss of a teleological sense. "Can one be a saint if God does not exist? That is the only concrete problem I know of today," wrote Albert Camus in *The Fall*.

Gary Varvel for the *Indianpolis Star*. Reprinted with permission.

Civilization holds together when a society learns to place moral values above the human appetites for power, wealth, violence, and pleasure. Historically, it has always relied on religion to provide a source for that moral authority. In fact, according to [historians] Will and Ariel Durant, "There is no significant example in history, before our time, of a society successfully maintaining moral life without the aid of religion." They added the foreboding remark, "The greatest question of our time is not communism versus individualism, not Europe versus America, not even the East versus the West; it is whether men can live without God."

[Playwright and former president of Czechoslovakia] Vàclav Havel, a survivor of a civilization that tried to live without God, sees the crisis clearly:

I believe that with the loss of God, man has lost a kind of absolute and universal system of coordinates, to which he could always relate everything, chiefly himself. His world and his personality gradually began to break up into separate, incoherent fragments corresponding to different, relative, coordinates.

On moral issues—social justice, sexuality, marriage and family, definitions of life and death—society badly needs a moral tether, or "system of coordinates" in Havel's phrase. Otherwise, our laws and politics will begin to reflect the same kind of moral schizophrenia already seen in individuals.

On what moral basis do doctrinaire Darwinians, committed to the survival of the fittest, ask us to protect the environment, in effect lending a hand to those we make "unfit"? On what basis do abortionists denounce the gender-based abortion practiced in India, where, in some cities, 99 percent of abortions involve a female fetus? (For this reason, some Indian cities have made it illegal for doctors to reveal to parents a fetus's gender after an ultrasound test.) Increasingly, the schizophrenia of personal morality is being projected onto society at large.

James Davison Hunter recounts watching a segment of the *Phil Donahue Show* featuring men who left their wives and then had affairs with those wives' mothers. Some of the relationships failed, but some worked out fine, the men reported. A psychologist sitting on the panel concluded, "The important thing to remember is that there is no right or wrong. I hear no wrongdoing. As I listen to their stories, I hear pain."

The Fate of a Godless Society

Hunter speculates where a society might be headed once it loses all moral consensus. "Personally I'm into ritual animal sacrifice," says one citizen. "Oh, really," says another. "I happen to be into man-boy relationships." "That's great," responds a third, "but my preference is . . ." and so on. The logical end of such thinking, Hunter suggests, can be found in the Marquis de Sade's novel *Juliette*, which declares, "Nothing is forbidden by nature."

In Sade's novel, Juliette's lover enhances their sexual ecstasy by raping Juliette's daughter and throwing the girl into a fire; wielding a poker, the mother herself prevents the child's escape. A brute accused of raping, sodomizing, and murdering more than two dozen boys, girls, men, and women defends himself by saying that all concepts of virtue and vice are arbitrary; self-interest is the paramount rule:

> Justice has no real existence, it is the deity of every passion. . . . So let us abandon our belief in this fiction, it no more exists than does the God of whom fools believe it the image; there is no God in this world, neither is there virtue, neither is there justice; there is nothing good, useful, or necessary but our passions.

U.S. courts today take pains to decide the merits of a case apart from religion or natural law. New York State passed a law prohibiting the use of children in pornographic films and, in order to protect it from civil libertarians, specified that the law is based not on moral or religious reasons, rather on "mental health" grounds. In earlier times the Supreme Court appealed to the "general consent" of society's moral values in deciding issues such as polygamy. I wonder on what possible grounds the Court might rule against polygamy today (practiced in 84 percent of all recorded cultures)—or incest, or pederasty, for that matter. All these moral taboos derive from a religious base; take away that foundation, and why should the practices be forbidden?

To ask a basic question, What sense does marriage make in a morally neutral society? A friend of mine, though gay, is nevertheless troubled by calls for gay marriages. "What's to keep two brothers from marrying, if they declare a commitment to each other?" he asks. "They could then enjoy the tax breaks and advantages of inheritance and health plans. It seems to me something more should be at stake in an institution like marriage." Yes, but *what* is at stake in marriage? The authors of *Habits of the Heart* found that few individuals in their survey except committed Christians could explain why they stayed married to their spouses. Marriage as a social construct is arbitrary, flexible, and open to redefinition. Marriage as a sacrament established by God is another matter entirely.

Separating Sex from Morality

Feminist thinkers have led the way in questioning the traditional basis of sexual ethics. In *The Erotic Silence of the American Wife*, Dalma Heyn argues that women unnaturally bind themselves at the marriage altar, abandoning their true needs and desires. Heyn recommends extramarital affairs as the cure for what she sardonically calls "the Donna Reed syndrome." In an essay in *Time*, Barbara Ehrenreich celebrated the fact that "Sex can finally, after all these centuries, be separated from the all-too-serious business of reproduction. . . . The only ethic that can work in an overcrowded world is one that insists that . . . sex—preferably among affectionate and consenting adults—belongs squarely in the realm of play."

Ehrenreich and Heyn are detaching sex from any teleological meaning invested in it by religion. But why limit the experience to affectionate and consenting adults? If sex is a matter of play, why not sanction pederasty, as did the Greeks and Romans? Why choose the age of 18—or 16, or 14, or 12—to mark an arbitrary distinction between child abuse and indulging in play? If sex is mere play, why do we prosecute people for incest? (Indeed, the Sex Information and Education Council of the United States circulated a paper expressing skepticism regarding "moral and religious pronouncements with respect to incest," lamenting that the taboo has hindered scientific investigation.)

The Alice-in-Wonderland world of untethered ethics has little place for traditional morality. When California adopted a sex-education program, the American Civil Liberties Union (ACLU) sent this official memorandum:

> The ACLU regrets to inform you of our opposition to SB 2394 concerning sex education in public schools. It is our position that teaching that monogamous, heterosexual intercourse within marriage is a traditional American value is an unconstitutional establishment of religious doctrine in public schools. . . . We believe SB 2394 violates the First Amendment.

Secularists Cannot Defend Any Morality

Again I stress, to me the question is not why modern secularists reject traditional morality, but on what grounds they defend any morality. Our legal system vigorously defends a woman's right to choose abortion—but why stop there? Historically, abandonment has been the more common means of disposing of unwanted children. Romans did it, Greeks did it, and during Rousseau's lifetime, one-third of babies in Paris were simply abandoned. Yet today, in the United States, if a mother leaves her baby in a Chicago alley, or two teens deposit their newborn in a Dempsey Dumpster, they are subject to prosecution.

We feel outrage when we hear of a middle-class couple "dumping" an Alzheimer's-afflicted parent when they no longer wish to care for him, or when kids push a five-year-old out the window of a high-rise building, or a ten-year-old is raped in a hallway, or a mother drowns her two children because they interfere with her lifestyle. Why? On what grounds do we feel outrage if we truly believe that morality is self-determined? Evidently the people who committed the crimes felt no compunction. And if morality is not, in the end, self-determined, who determines it? On what basis do we decide?

In the landmark book *Faith in the Future*, Jonathan Sacks, chief rabbi of the United Hebrew Congregations of the (British) Commonwealth, argues that human society was meant to be a covenant between God and humankind, a collaborative enterprise based on common values and vision. Instead, it has become "an aggregate of individuals pursuing private interest, coming together temporarily and contractually, and leaving the state to resolve their conflicts on value-neutral grounds." In the process, "the individual loses his moorings . . . and becomes prone to a sense of meaninglessness and despair." Sacks argues that only by restoring the "moral covenant" can we reverse the breakdown in the social fabric of Western civilization.

Or, as the Jewish medical educator David C. Stolinsky put it, "The reason we fear to go out after dark is not that we may be set upon by bands of evangelicals and forced to read the New Testament, but that we may be set upon by gangs of feral young people who have been taught that nothing is superior to their own needs or feelings.". . .

The Absolute Value of Individuals

In his study *Morality: Religious and Secular*, Basil Mitchell argues that, since the eighteenth century, secular thinkers have attempted to make reason, not religion, the basis of morality. None has successfully found a way to establish an *absolute* value for the individual human person. Mitchell suggests that secular thinkers can establish a relative value for people, by comparing people to animals, say, or to each other; but the idea that every person has an absolute value came out of Christianity and Judaism before it and is absent from every other ancient philosophy or religion.

The Founding Fathers of the United States, apparently aware of the danger, made a valiant attempt to connect individual rights to a transcendent source. Overruling Thomas Jefferson, who had made only a vague reference to "the Laws of Nature and of Nature's God," they insisted instead on including the words "unalienable" and "endowed by their Creator." They did so in order to secure such rights in a transcendent Higher Power, so that no human power could attempt to take them away. Human dignity and worth derive from God's.

Yet if there is no Creator to endow these rights, on what basis can they be considered unalienable? Precisely that question is asked openly today. Robert Jarvik, a scientist and inventor of the artificial human heart, expresses the more modern view:

> In reality, there are no basic human rights. Mankind created them. They are conventions we agree to abide by for our mutual protection under law. Are there basic animal rights? Basic plant rights? Basic rights of any kind to protect things on our planet when the sun eventually burns out, or when we block it out with radioactive clouds? Someday, humans will realize that we are a part of nature and not separate from it. We have no more basic rights than viruses, other than those that we create for ourselves through our intellect and our compassion.

Jarvik captures the dilemma: If humans are not made in the image of God, somehow distinct from animals, what gives us any more rights than other species? Some animal rights activists already ask that question, and a writer in the journal *Wild Earth* even mused about the logical consequences:

> If you haven't given voluntary human extinction much thought before, the idea of a world with no people may seem strange. But, if you give the idea a chance I think you might agree that the extinction of *Homo sapiens* would mean survival

44

for millions, if not billions, of other Earth-dwelling species. . . . Phasing out the human race will solve every problem on earth, social and environmental.

When representatives from the United States meet with their counterparts from China and Singapore to hammer out an agreement on human rights, not only do they have no common ground, they have no self-coherent ground on which to stand. Our founders made human dignity an irreducible value rooted in creation, a dignity that exists prior to any "public" status as citizen. Eliminate the Creator, and everything is on the negotiating table. By destroying the link between the social and cosmic orders, we have effectively destroyed the validity of the social order.

> *"Something is not moral because God commands it, but rather because it successfully fits the needs of a human society."*

Religion Is Not Essential to a Moral Society

Dave Matson

Dave Matson states in the following viewpoint that morality exists independently of God or religion. He argues that moral laws, such as those that prohibit murder and theft, were created by humans so that society could function peacefully and efficiently. While some moral laws vary according to the needs of specific societies, Matson contends, the one universal standard of morality is empathy for others, and this standard holds true for atheists as well as believers. Matson has authored a variety of articles for the *Skeptical Review* and the *Freethought Exchange*. He is also the editor of the Oak Hill Free Press.

As you read, consider the following questions:
1. How does morality promote cooperation, as explained by Matson?
2. According to the author, why doesn't the Bible set the standard for morality?
3. Why does Matson believe that moral rules would be enforced even if there were no God?

Excerpted from "The Law of the Jungle," by Dave Matson, *Skeptical Review*, no. 3, 1994. Reprinted with the permission of the author and *Skeptical Review*. The author can be reached at 103514.3640@compuserve.com.

Once upon a time, in the bad old days, ancestor Mitchell became annoyed with ancestor Till. Since there were no moral laws then, ancestor Mitchell decided to act on his anger. Thus, one fine morning, he gathered together his hunting buddies and savaged ancestor Till's household. Many of ancestor Till's relatives were killed and ancestor Till was staked out for the vultures. Since there were no laws then, life went on as before. Then, one fine morning, when many of ancestor Mitchell's friends were out hunting mammoths, ancestor Mitchell's household was ravaged. Many of his family were killed and ancestor Mitchell was staked out for the vultures.

In the months that followed, there were raids and counterraids and the violence spread throughout the campsites and caves. Every man kept one eye on his neighbors and one hand on his war club, which made it hard to sleep or have any fun. Worse, a neighboring tribe, sensing their internal disorder, moved in on their favorite mammoth hunting grounds! There were no happy campers in that neck of the woods. Nobody was benefiting from this arrangement except the vultures!

One hot day the grumbling got so bad that some surviving sons of ancestor Till and ancestor Mitchell got together and declared a truce. The importance of upholding the truce was so great that each side threatened to exile any of its own members who broke it. It was better to lose one man than to endanger everyone. Thus, the first moral law was made: Thou shall not kill a fellow tribesman. Soon, another law was made to prevent theft, a situation that often led to killing. Still other laws were made to allow for cooperation on the hunt and for mutual defense. Thus, there was less fighting over mammoths and other goods. Soon the old hunting grounds had been won back, and everyone in that group had the same sense of right and wrong in large and small matters. Without having to watch their backs constantly, and with laws and conventions to minimize friction and handle incidents, the Till people and the Mitchell people worked together efficiently on complex projects and prospered. Their moral laws were not perfect, but they were good enough to get the job done.

The point of our little story, which is not intended as a scientific reconstruction, is that morality is the grease that allows a group to function. People simply cannot live together and do as they please any more than city drivers can ignore all the traffic rules. Chaos would set in, and the tribe would soon fall apart or be conquered by its neighbors.

Morality Promotes Cooperation

Morality was born in efficient communal living, and that is where we must initially seek its meaning. It's no accident that the very qualities of moral behavior relate to life within a group. Kindness, sympathy, honesty, generosity, mercy, loyalty, justice, and courage are qualities that strengthen the group. Even courage, which may apply to a hermit, takes its highest moral form in a group. Morality is, therefore, concerned with minimizing disruption within the group and, equally important, promoting cooperation. Efficient cooperation, in turn, requires justice. Nobody's going to cooperate on the next mammoth hunt if he is constantly cheated of his fair share! Thus, we see the origins of morality and justice.

Animal communities, each according to their particular needs, must also obey moral "laws" and conventions in order to function efficiently. Therefore, it should not surprise you to learn that many animals exhibit some fine moral traits that would put many humans to shame. It is beyond the scope of this viewpoint to go into the fascinating world of animal morality, but its mere existence is another proof that morality originates in the needs of a group.

Whether we're dealing with animal or human societies, keep in mind that not every society has found ideal moral solutions. Some societies grind along less smoothly than others. Some limp along, their demise likely. The insights into morality are not in the particulars but rather in the general landscape. Having briefly traced some of the major threads defining morality, we see that morality is neither entirely relative nor completely fixed. No doubt there are many different rules that would work beautifully for any given society. Furthermore, the needs of a jungle or tropical island society are not the same as those of a European society, and even in cases where similar rules might apply there is no guarantee that similar conventions would be adopted if several good solutions exist. Thus, an island society might go about in the buff whereas a Victorian society would be shocked by such behavior. One society might allow premarital sex while another condemns it. To that extent morality is relative to specific societies.

Yet, there is a core of common bedrock to morality. The basic needs of all societies are quite similar inasmuch as the basic human needs are similar. Murder and theft, with possible ritual exceptions, have no place in any well ordered society. Harmfulness in any form, within the group, is invariably frowned upon. Good behavior towards others in the group is an asset. How you rate with your hunting buddies could be really important the next time you're cornered by that tiger! Thus, in a healthy society, morality is never a case of "anything goes." To that extent, even though the boundaries are a bit fuzzy, we may say that morality is absolute.

Thus, having explored the rudiments of morality, we must extend it to all of mankind. The great moralists have seen that the tribal boundaries are, in the final analysis, an artificial division between human beings. Why should morality be limited to one's tribe? If there is a great truth here it must be a universal one. We must not do to others what is hurtful to ourselves unless it is to prevent a greater physical harm. Tribal good manners must now apply to everyone if humanity is to be one, happy family. Let those who would allot happiness to a select portion of humanity live among the deprived!

The Universal Principle of Empathy

On a deeper level, it is ignorance that separates human from human, and humans from animals. If we could but perfectly understand the feelings and thoughts and dreams of our fellow man, even as we learn that absolute truth is not our personal property, we would see that the boundary between him and us is very faint, that to harm him is very much like harming ourselves, that to help him is very much like helping ourselves. This natural sympathy, this empathy for our fellow man, is the keystone in the arch of morality whose foundations are anchored in the needs of the group. It allows us to see morality as a universal principle that, in its ultimate form, takes in all thinking creatures according to their needs.

This great arch of morality is built out of stones we can see. There are no supernatural elements in it. According to Kai Nielsen, "A man who says, 'If God is dead, nothing matters,' is a spoilt child who has never looked at his fellowman with compassion." To look at our fellowman with compassion is to understand his feelings, needs, and dreams, to walk a mile in his shoes, to become as one through empathy.

Being rooted in the human tribal condition, morality can never be simply what God commands. That is, something is not moral because God commands it, but rather because it successfully fits the needs of a human society. Thus, once man becomes God's chief concern, moral law is largely fixed and independent of God himself. God, knowing the human condition, is free to choose among those moral rules that will work, but he can never be the standard. . . .

Morality Originates in the Human Condition

We may consign to oblivion the claim, so often heard, that atheists have no standard of morality. Indeed, as you can now see, they draw from the same standard as the most devoted Bible-believer! The chief difference is that the Bible-believer is confused as to morality's true origin and, as a result, may commit atrocities in "the name of God." Again, morality originates in the human condition and not in divine edicts, and the man or woman who realizes that has the clearest compass to travel life's moral highways.

We may consign to oblivion the claim, so often heard, that the Bible sets the standard for morality. No book can set the standard for morality. At best, a book might illuminate workable principles that can be discovered by other means. Many cultural roads lead to morality. The Japanese, for example, are a highly moral people despite being unfamiliar with the Bible.

We may consign to oblivion the claim, so often heard, that "anything goes" without God. Since moral rules are rooted in the smooth functioning of a society, they will be enforced even if there were no God. Do as you please, and you go directly to jail! (Do not collect $200.) Rulers, even bad ones, would no more dispense with morality in general (inside their own societies) than they would dispense with traffic rules. Societies, of course, can become perverted to various degrees. Indeed, past Christian societies have some of the blackest records of all. A belief in Jesus offers no magical cure, as any good historian of Christianity can tell you.

Give me your tired, your poor, the wretched refuse
of your teeming shore – provided they have
been baptized in the name of
The Father, and of The Son, and of The Holy Ghost.

Ann E. Zindler. Reprinted by permission of American Atheist Press.

We may consign to oblivion the claim, so often heard, that God cannot be judged on moral matters by mere humans. We might imagine that God is very wise, that he knows far more than we ever could hope to know, but that doesn't mean we know nothing. We do know something about our world!

Consider a chess game in progress. On one side of the board sits God, a Grandmaster whose skill we wood pushers could never hope to equal. You (a mere human) are his opponent. Although your knowledge is nowhere near that of the Grandmaster, it does not follow that you know nothing about chess. Indeed, there are many positions you could win even against the Grandmaster. Should this Grandmaster allow such a position, you would rightly judge his game to be lost. In charges of gross immorality, it is no defense to claim that God is so much higher than we are that we cannot hope to know what he's up to. We do have a pretty good idea of what morality is all about! Human morality deals with conditions down here on Earth—not those of inscrutable heaven. Thus, if an action appears grossly immoral with no obvious, compensating circumstances, then there *is* no adequate defense.

The idea that God might have to do a great harm in order to insure a greater good is no defense. It makes God out to be a weakling! [One writer], for example, suggests the possibility that God might have looked down the long corridor of time and seen "that the babes of Amalek were destined to become vicious beasts like their ancestors." God winds up with great eyesight but no brains! Whatever happened to retraining? If God is all-wise and all-good and all-powerful, then retraining the Amalekites could not have posed a problem to him. Indeed, we might expect God to do even better than that! There must be dozens of solutions that are infinitely better than butchering all the women and children.

God Has No Claim to Morality

One might urge that God, being no part of any human society, is free to do as he pleases. However, an all-powerful being with perfect empathy towards creatures he needlessly torments can have no claim to morality. Such is the description of a fiend. We don't need a second opinion about torturing children for fun. If it's evil for us to do it, then it's no less evil if a king—or a god—does it. The evil of an act lies in its consequences, its hurt, not in who does it. One's only hope would be that a sufficiently powerful being did it to bring about a greater good that was hidden from the rest of us. Unfortunately, the greater the agent's power, the less need there is for a hurt-now-enjoy-later solution. Thus, the theist, whose God is absolutely powerful, is deprived of his only escape hatch.

If the slaughter of the Amalekites were done without God's orders, then we would immediately judge it to be a gross act of immorality. That would be a clear violation of a universal morality whose basic nature we worked out earlier. Indeed, the particular crime suggests that the participants have not evolved beyond the primitive, tribal concept of morality.

To make God the author of this act does nothing to lessen its immorality. Since God is all-powerful, he is deprived of his only possible defense, i.e., needing to commit a harm to reach a greater good. Therefore, since we have an adequate understanding of morality, to whose standards even God is not exempt, we may say that if God directed the massacre of Amalekite men, women, children, and babies—and even the animals—then he stands convicted of gross immorality.

| "*Stable, intact families make a vital contribution to the nurturing of communities and citizens.*"

Society's Well-Being Depends upon the Traditional Family

Jean Bethke Elshtain

In the following viewpoint, Jean Bethke Elshtain asserts that the two-parent family is crucial to the well-being of America's children and society as a whole. In Elshtain's view, divorce and single parenthood contributes to a wide array of social problems, including teen suicide, crime, drug abuse, and poverty. She contends that marriage provides the only environment in which children can truly flourish. Elshtain is a professor of Social and Political Ethics at the University of Chicago's Divinity School.

As you read, consider the following questions:

1. In what ways does family breakdown negatively impact children's lives, in the author's view?
2. What is the best antipoverty program for children, according to Elshtain?
3. As explained by Elshtain, what lessons do families teach?

Excerpted from "Families and Citizens: Why the Stakes of Democracy Are So High," speech given by Jean Bethke Elshtain, February 16, 1995, in Minneapolis. Available at www.amexp.org/publications/culture/culture18.htm. Reprinted with permission from the author.

In their November 1993 pastoral message, "Follow the Way of Love," the Catholic Bishops reminded us that: "The family exists at the heart of all societies. It is the first and most basic community to which every person belongs. There is nothing more fundamental to our vitality as a society and as a church for, in the words of Pope John Paul II, 'the future of humanity passes by way of the family.'"

Agreeing as I do with the Bishops in this matter, it is my solemn duty to report that the status of the family is very troubled indeed. On *every* index of well-being, the quality of life for America's children is declining. Indeed, it must be said that American children are more and more in peril because they are less and less assured of the sustained care, support and safety that comes only with order and nurturance in their immediate environments. Children are bearing the brunt of a profound cultural shift whose negative features we are now in a position to observe and whose continuing costs will last much longer than our own lifetimes. It is my hope that renewed attention to the declining status of the family, perhaps because the evidence of wreckage is visible to even the most insouciant among us, will help to forestall further destruction.

I have been in the front lines of the family debate, as it is sometimes called, for nearly two decades. I can assure you that it has not been easy. A defense of the two-parent family and the need for children to be reared in a situation of trust, intimacy, fidelity and security was regarded by many, and called by some, a reactionary position. I submit to you that the experiment in loosening up the ties that bind has been tried and that it has failed. It has failed our children; it has failed our parents; and it has failed our society.

A Whole Range of Troubles for Children

There is a high correlation between broken homes and a whole range of troubles for children. Three out of four teenage suicides occur in households where a parent has been absent. Eighty percent of adolescents in psychiatric hospitals come from broken homes. Tracking studies report that five out of six adolescents caught up in the criminal justice system come from families where a parent (usually the father) is absent. A 1988 government survey of 17,000 children found that children living apart from a biological parent are 20 to 40 percent more vulnerable to sickness. Out-of-wedlock births are nearing 80 percent in some inner-city neighborhoods where family disintegration is most severe.

Recent reports indicate that every day in America over 500 children, ages 10 to 14, begin using illegal drugs and over 1,000 start drinking alcohol. Among 15- to 19-year-olds, homicide by firearms is the third leading cause of death after motor vehicle accidents and suicide. Murder is the leading cause of death for young African-Americans and those who kill them are themselves young black men. This is just one small snippet of the overall and increasingly grim picture.

Let me lift up for your consideration just one additional statistic, this from a document called the "Kids Count Data Book" issued by the Casey Foundation. What researchers learned was startling. But, before I report the data, let me suggest that these findings help to support the call for a dramatic change in the way in which we think about the family and its troubles. One view, widely held, is that poverty is the leading cause of family disintegration, breakdown and troubles for children. It has seemed to many of us for a long time that this is too simple a picture of what is going on. In fact, we have suggested that cultural transformation itself fuels poverty and other social and economic problems. Now to the figures.

Two groups were compared. In one group, the couple—a young man and woman, completed high school; got married; and waited until age 20 to have a child. In the second group, none of those things happened. The biological mother and father did not marry; neither one completed high school; and a child was born before the mother was 20 years old. In the first group, with high school completion and marriage, only eight percent of the children are in poverty. In the second group, where high school was not completed and marriage was eschewed, fully 79 percent of these children are in poverty. What these figures suggest is that the best anti-poverty program for children is a stable, intact, two-parent family. Changes in family structure over the past generation are strongly correlated with rising rates of poverty among children.

Consider another example. We have known for a long time that divorce under current laws often spells economic hardship, even disaster, for custodial parents and their minor children. A widespread "culture of divorce" does precious little to sustain couples through periods of marital turmoil. The current slight decline in the divorce rate is one small ray of hope. But what most needs attention is the post-divorce situation in child-rearing households and, perhaps even more importantly, rebuilding and reweaving the threads of community in order to encourage young people to marry before they have children.

My status report to you begins, then, with an insistence on the importance of mothers and fathers to the life of child, church, and community. In light of the undeniable evidence of family breakdown and deinstitutionalization, especially the severing of basic parental ties, it is enormously disturbing to read and listen to those who, despite all the evidence, continue to paint a rosy picture of "change" and "readjustment," and who refuse to confront the actual situation in which America's parents and children find themselves. The decline in the well-being of America's children is directly traceable to the stresses and strains which undermine the family as an ethical entity that, in the words of political philosopher William Galston, "transmits or fails to transmit the beliefs and dispositions needed to support oneself and to contribute to one's community."

Family Matters

The status of the family matters because there are a range of tasks that families undertake that cannot be delegated satisfactorily to other institutions. Stable, intact families make a vital contribution to the nurturing of communities and citizens. More and more teachers, for example, complain that they cannot do their job as teachers because frustrated, angry, lonely children "act out," behaving violently towards classmates and teachers; or, alternately, they are "clingy" because they lack parental guidance and comfort. This prevents children from working on reading, writing and arithmetic. We see, once again, that family breakdown fuels other troubles.

This assessment received powerful confirmation recently

as a result of a study comparing parents' and teachers' ratings of more than 2,000 children from ages seven to 16. The study showed that emotional and behavioral problems have been increasing since the mid-1970s for American children. As the *New York Times* reported, of 118 specific problems and abilities assessed, there was a significant worsening in 45, including withdrawal; immaturity and overdependency; inability to concentrate or being too nervous to concentrate; aggressivity (including lying, cheating, meanness to others, destroying other people's things, disobedience); temperamental outbursts and incessant demands for attention; anxiety and depression, as well as feeling unloved, nervous, sad, and depressed.

This is terrible. Dr. Thomas Achenbach, Director of the Center for Children, Youth, and Families at the University of Vermont, comments, "It's not the magnitude of the changes, but the consistency that is so significant." He goes on to aver that there are "probably multiple factors behind such a widespread increase in problems." But he especially cites "less parental monitoring of what kids are doing, less time with parents because there are more single-parent families [as well as] families with both parents working. . . ." As a result, schools are having to cope with noneducational issues, like discipline, making it harder for them to fulfill their basic mission. We come back, again, to the underlying problem that fuels other difficulties: The breakdown of the family.

Common Testimony

This enables us to see quite clearly that, although the family is the locus of private life, it is also critical to public life, to the life of community and civic associations. Here the testimony of parents and experts converges. When parents are asked to tell their own version of our current discontents, they lament the fact that it is harder to do a decent job raising children in a culture that is unfriendly to families and family attachments. A culture that mocks those who raise questions about the wisdom of celebrating single-parent households is scarcely a culture prepared to look at the Smith family in Fremont, Nebraska, and say to Betty and Bob, "Well done. Keep at it. We're with you. We are supporting you in your effort." The overwhelming majority of Americans, between 80–88 percent, believe that being a parent is much more difficult that it used to be. Pessimism about the decline of family values is increasing, especially among women and Hispanic and African-American citizens.

The Importance of Marriage

The heart of family life is marriage, the foundation of civilization. Marriage, which brings the two sexes together in a unique legal, social, economic, and spiritual union, has had special protection within the law and the culture because it is indispensable to civilized life.

No other relationship provides society what marriage does. No other relationship transforms young men and women into more productive, less selfish and more mature husbands and wives, and fathers and mothers, than marriage. No other relationship affords children the best economic, emotional and psychological environment. Only as we have drifted from the defense of marriage have we experienced soaring social problems, such as divorce, illegitimacy, sexually-transmitted diseases, and crime. The answer is not to push the envelope further but to restore the primacy of marriage within the law and the culture.

Robert H. Knight, *Family Research Council*, March 12, 1997.

While the debate of experts and advocates over the past several decades has tended to focus on how to get both parents into full-time work, or how to fund child care given the fact that both parents are in full-time work, the grassroots conversation revolves around cultural values. Parents express a pervasive fear that they have less time to spend in the ethical task of child-rearing and that, as a result, their children are succumbing to the values of a culture parents view as excessively individualistic and materialistic.

Let me offer one other piece of testimony, this from a taxicab ride I took recently in Washington, D.C., heading from the capitol to National Airport. My taxi driver was a Nigerian woman who had come here with her family some eight years ago. She told me that she was hoping to return to Nigeria because American culture was destroying her family. She said to me, as I took notes in the back of the cab,

"If they don't tidy that mess up, you can forget it. Where there is no family structure, kids don't have to answer to anybody. America has to tidy this up! All this lack of discipline. The kids get dumped. We can't even salvage our own kids."

She went on to tell me that her 13-year-old son had been caught using drugs and that her 11-year-old daughter had taunted her recently, during the course of a disagreement, "When I'm 12 years old, I'll have a baby and I'll be on my own." My taxi-driver witness, shaking her head, said angrily: "The baby becomes the job; then the second baby is the promotion. Things now are so terrible. I'm sure all this was set up in good faith, but now everything seems to be going wrong."

The time is surely right to bring together the concerns of parents and of witnesses on the street with the evidence and analyses of experts. Both scholarly and public opinion now converge on the conclusion that our children are in trouble and, according to the National Commission on Children, those growing up in single-parent households are at greater risk than those in two-parent households for poverty, substance abuse, adolescent childbearing, criminality, suicide, mental illness, and dropping out of school. Why should this surprise us? Families teach us our first lessons in responsibility and reciprocity. Writes Ernesto Cortez, Jr., head of the Texas Industrial Areas Foundation Network, in a piece on the Catholic tradition of family rights:

> Families teach the first lessons of relationships among persons, some of which are essential not only to private life but to public life as well. Within the family, one learns to act upon others and to be acted upon. It is in the family that we learn to identify ourselves with others or fail to learn to love. It is in the family that we learn to give and take with others—or fail to learn to be reciprocal. It is in the family that we learn to trust others as we depend on them or learn to distrust them. We learn to form expectations of others and to hold them accountable. We also learn to hold ourselves accountable. These lessons of reciprocity, trust, discipline, and self-restraint are important to the forming of relationships in public life.

This family is not an isolated unit but very much a social institution, nested in a wider surround, that either helps to sustain parental commitment and accomplishments or puts negative pressure on mothers and fathers. That pressure obviously takes many forms and I have mentioned just a few. Being a parent isn't just another lifestyle choice. It is an ethical vocation of the weightiest sort. Communities, including churches, should lighten the burden and smooth the path for parents in order that the complex joys of family life might rise to the surface, and in order that the undeniable burdens of family responsibility might be more openheartedly borne.

Our Capacity for Human Sociality

Children lost to society in increasing numbers may be a growing phenomenon, but it is one we must name for what it is: a loss, a crying shame. Protecting, preserving, and strengthening family autonomy and the well-being of mothers and fathers is a way of affirming our commitment to the individual and to that democratic society that best speaks to the aspirations of individuals. The rights of persons are fundamentally social. What is at stake in the family debate and our response to it is nothing less than our capacity for human sociality.

To mutter blithe nostrums about "choice" and "independent motherhood" when our eyes should be on the 14-year-old crack-addicted, undereducated, pregnant girl living in a disintegrating and violent neighborhood, rather than the glamorous "Murphy Brown," is both cruel and contemptuous, although in the American academy today this sometimes gets presented as the liberal thing to do or to say. It is not. It is illiberal in the extreme, if by liberal we mean generous, openhanded, and not bound by prefabricated tenets. Only the most rigid of individualistic orthodoxies can celebrate single-motherhood as good for either women or children. Creating a norm out of what is a tremendous burden and, in the vast majority of cases, an unwelcome reality, is a strategy of evasion—indeed, of repudiating what a preferential option for the child requires.

Taking this latter tack, we are well-advised to begin with a covenanted view of marital commitment in which we all have a stake, as parents, as citizens, and, undeniably, as children of God. Given the dismal status of the family, I would hope that over the next decade in American society we could set aside sterile disputes and get down to the business of confronting the wider crisis of values. For make no mistake about it, the problem of values lies at the heart of the matter—not poverty, not crime, not the lack of day care, but values. That fuels all the other issues and all the other problems.

| *"Family values' requires 'valuing families,'
| *no matter what their form—traditional,
| *extended, two-parent, one-parent."*

Society's Well-Being Does Not Depend upon the Traditional Family

Arlene Skolnick and Stacey Rosencrantz

In the following viewpoint, Arlene Skolnick and Stacey Rosencrantz refute claims that the traditional nuclear family is the only successful family structure. According to the authors, the notion that most social problems are caused by "the breakdown of the family" relies on flawed research that exaggerates the negative effects of divorce on children. Skolnick and Rosencrantz argue that the most important determinant of a child's well-being is not a two-parent family, but a close relationship with one parent. Skolnick is a research psychologist at the Institute of Human Development, University of California, Berkeley, and the author of *Embattled Paradise: The American Family in an Age of Uncertainty*. Rosencrantz was a graduate student in Stanford University's psychology department at the time this viewpoint was written.

As you read, consider the following questions:
1. In Skolnick and Rosencrantz's opinion, what questions must be answered before society can determine which policies would improve the well-being of children?
2. What methodological problems of divorce research are mentioned by the authors?
3. According to the authors, why is the "language of moral decay" inadequate to discuss American families?

Excerpted from "The New Crusade for the Old Family," by Arlene Skolnick and Stacey Rosencrantz, *The American Prospect*, vol.18, Summer 1994. Copyright ©1994 by The American Prospect. Reprinted with the permission of *The American Prospect*.

What is the root cause in America of poverty, crime, drug abuse, gang warfare, urban decay, and failing schools? According to op-ed pundits, Sunday talking heads, radio call-in shows, and politicians in both parties, the answer is the growing number of children being raised by single parents, especially by mothers who never married in the first place. Restore family values and the two-parent family, and America's social problems will be substantially solved.

By the close of the 1992 presidential campaign, the war over family values seemed to fade. Dan Quayle's attack on Murphy Brown's single motherhood stirred more ridicule on late night talk shows than moral panic. The public clearly preferred Bill Clinton's focus on the economy and his more inclusive version of the family theme: "family values" means "valuing families," no matter what their form—traditional, extended, two-parent, one-parent.

Yet Clinton's victory was quickly followed by a new bipartisan crusade to restore the two-parent family by discouraging divorce as well as out-of-wedlock childbearing. The conservative right has for years equated family values with the traditional image of the nuclear family. The new crusade drew people from across the spectrum—Democrats as well as Republicans, conservatives, liberals, and communitarians. Eventually, even President Clinton joined in, remarking that he had reread Quayle's speech and "found a lot of good things in it."

While the new family restorationists do not agree on a program for reducing the number of single-parent families, they generally use a language of moral failure and cultural decline to account for family change. Many want to revive the stigma that used to surround divorce and single motherhood. To change the cultural climate, they call for government and media campaigns like those that have discouraged smoking and drinking. They propose to make divorce harder or slower or even, as the late Christopher Lasch proposed, to outlaw divorce by parents with minor children. . . .

The Divisive Rhetoric of Family Values

Focusing attention on the needs and problems of families raising children could be enormously positive. But the current crusade draws on the family values scripts of the 1980s, posing the issue in a divisive way (Are you against the two-parent family?) and painting critics into an anti-family corner. Restricting legal channels for divorce, cutting off welfare to unmarried mothers, and restoring the old censorious attitudes toward single parenthood may harm many children and deepen the very social ills we are trying to remedy.

There's nothing new in blaming social problems on "the breakdown of the family" or in making the "fallen woman" and her bastard child into objects of scorn and pity. Throughout our history, public policies made divorce difficult to obtain and penalized unwed parents and often their children. In the 1960s and 1970s, however, public opinion turned more tolerant and legal systems throughout the West became unwilling to brand some children as "illegitimate" and deprive them of rights due others. Now we are being told that this new tolerance was a mistake.

Most Americans, even those most committed to greater equality between women and men, are deeply uneasy about recent family changes and worried about crime and violence. The new case for the old family owes much of its persuasive power to the authority of social science. "The evidence is in," declares Barbara Dafoe Whitehead, author of a much-discussed article, "Dan Quayle Was Right," which appeared in the April 1993 *Atlantic Monthly*. Divorce and single-parent families, Whitehead argues, are damaging both children and the social fabric. Another family restorationist, Karl Zinsmeister, a fellow at the American Enterprise Institute, refers to "a mountain of evidence" showing that children of divorce end up intellectually, physically, and emotionally scarred for life.

Despite these strong claims of scientific backing, the research literature is far more complicated than the family restorationists have let on. Whitehead says, "The debate about family structure is not simply about the social-scientific evidence. It is also a debate over deeply held and often conflicting values." Unfortunately, the family restorationists' values have colored their reading of the evidence.

Important Questions About Family

Few would deny that the divorce of one's parents is a painful experience and that children blessed with two "good enough" parents generally have an easier time growing up than others. Raising a child from infancy to successful adulthood can be a daunting task even for two people. But to decide what policies would improve children's lives, we need to answer a number of prior questions:

- Are children who grow up in a one-parent home markedly worse off than those who live with both parents?
- If such children are so disadvantaged, is the source of their problems family structure or some other factor that may have existed earlier or be associated with it?
- How effectively can public policies promote a particular form of family and discourage others? Will policies intended to stigmatize and reduce or prevent divorce or single parenthood cause unintended harm to children's well-being? Would positive measures to help single-parent families or reduce the stress that accompanies marital disruption be of more benefit to children?

Finally, is there a direct link, as so many believe, between family structure and what a *Newsweek* writer calls a "nauseating buffet" of social pathologies, especially crime, violence, and drugs? In his Murphy Brown speech, given in the wake of the Los Angeles riots, Quayle argued that it wasn't poverty but a "poverty of values" that had led to family breakdown, which in turn caused the violence. The one sentence about Murphy Brown in the speech—borrowed incidentally from an op-ed by Whitehead—overshadowed the rest of the message. Charles Murray was more successful at linking family values with fear of crime. In a *Wall Street Journal* article, he warned that because of rising white illegitimacy rates, a "coming white underclass" was going to engulf the rest of society in the kind of anarchy found in the inner cities. But what is the evidence for this incendiary claim? And why do countries with similar trends in family structure not suffer from the social deterioration that plagues us?

The family restorationists do not provide clear answers to these questions. And the answers found in the research literature do not support their extreme statements about the consequences of family structure or some of the drastic policies they propose to change it.

Of course, it's always possible to raise methodological questions about a line of research or to interpret findings in more ways than one. The perfect study, like the perfect crime, is an elusive goal. But some of the family restorationists seem to misunderstand the social science enterprise in ways that seriously undermine their conclusions. For example, they trumpet findings about correlations between family structure and poverty, or lower academic achievement, or behavior problems, as proof of their arguments. Doing so, however, ignores the principle taught in elementary statistics that correlation does not prove causation.

For example, suppose we find that increased ice cream consumption is correlated with increases in drownings. The cause, of course, has nothing to do with ice cream but everything to do with the weather: people swim more and eat more ice cream in the summer. Similarly, single parenthood may be correlated with many problems affecting children, but the causes may lie elsewhere—for example, in economic and emotional problems affecting parents that lead to difficulties raising children and greater chances of divorce. Making it hard for such parents to divorce may no more improve the children's lives than banning ice cream would reduce drowning. Also, causation can and often does go in two directions. Poor women are more likely to have out-of-wedlock babies—this is one of the oldest correlates of poverty—but raising the child may impede them from escaping poverty. In short, finding a correlation between two variables is only a starting point for further analysis.

The Flawed Research of Family Restorationists

The social science research itself is also plagued by methodological problems. Most available studies of divorce, for example, are based on well-educated white families; some are based on families who have sought clinical help or become embroiled in legal conflict. Such families may hardly be representative. Comparing one study with one another is notoriously difficult because they use different measures to assess children of different ages after differing periods have elapsed since the divorce. Some studies, such as Judith Wallerstein's widely cited work on the harm of divorce reported in the

1989 book *Second Chances* by Wallerstein and Sandra Blakeslee, use no comparison groups at all. Others compare divorced families with intact families—both happy and unhappy—when a more appropriate comparison would be with couples that are unhappily married.

In addition, the family restorationists and some researchers lump together children of divorce and children whose parents never married. Yet never-married mothers are generally younger, poorer, and less educated than divorced mothers. And by some measures children living with never-married mothers are worse off than those living in divorced families.

The restorationists paint a far darker and more simplistic picture of the impact of divorce on children than does the research literature. Researchers agree that around the time their parents separate almost all children go through a period of distress. Within two or three years, most have recovered. The great majority of children of divorce do not appear to be impaired in their development. While some children do suffer lasting harm, the family restorationists exaggerate the extent and prevalence of long-term effects. For example, they may state that children of divorce face twice or three times the psychological risk of children in intact families. But the doubling of a risk may mean an increase from 2 to 4 percent, 10 to 20 percent, or from 30 to 60 percent. The effects of divorce tend to be in the smaller range.

In fact, a meta-analysis of divorce findings published in 1991 in the *Psychological Bulletin* reported very small differences between children from divorced and intact families in such measures of well-being as school achievement, psychological adjustment, self concept, and relations with parents and peers. (A "meta-analysis" combines data from separate studies into larger samples to make the findings more reliable.) Further, the more methodologically sophisticated studies—that is, those that controlled for other variables such as as income and parental conflict—reported the smallest differences.

The Impact of Divorce on Children

In general, researchers who interview or observe children of divorce report more findings of distress than those who use data from large sample surveys. Yet even in the clinical studies the majority of children develop normally. One point that researchers agree on is that children vary greatly in response to divorce, depending on their circumstances, age, and psychological traits and temperament.

The Traditional Family Is Not Superior

Harping on the superiority of married biological parents and the evils of fatherlessness injures children and parents in a wide array of contemporary families, including the millions of children who live with gay or lesbian parents. . . .

Nearly three decades of research finds gay and lesbian parents to be at least as successful as heterosexuals. Dozens of studies conclude that children reared by lesbian or gay parents have no greater gender or social difficulties than other children, except for the problems caused by homophobia and discrimination. Ironically, some of the worst risks these children suffer stem from our failure to legally recognize the actual two-parent families in which many live. . . .

It is time to face the irreversible historical fact that family diversity is here to stay. Of course, two good parents of whatever gender generally are better than one. But no one lives in a "general" family. Our unique, often imperfect, real families assume many shapes, sizes, and characters. Each type of family has strengths, vulnerabilities, and challenges, and each needs support and deserves respect. We can't coerce or preach people into successful marital or parenting relationships, but we can help them to succeed in the ones they form. What we need to promote instead of divisive self-righteous family values are inclusive, democratic, and compassionate *social* values.

Judith Stacey, *UTNE Reader*, September/October 1996.

Where differences between children of divorce and those in stable two-parent families show up, they may be due, not to the divorce itself, but to circumstances before, during, and after the legal undoing of the marital bond. Most researchers now view divorce not as a single event but as an unfolding process. The child will usually endure parental conflict, estrangement, and emotional upset, separation from one parent, and economic deprivation. Often divorce means moving away from home, neighborhood, and school.

Particular children may go through more or fewer such jolts than others.

Researchers have known for some time that children from intact homes with high conflict between the parents often have similar or even worse problems than children of divorced parents. Recent studies in this country as well as in Australia and Sweden confirm that marital discord between the parents is a major influence on children's well-being, whether or not a divorce occurs.

Some of the family restorationists recognize that children in high-conflict families might be better off if their parents divorced than if they stayed together. They want to discourage or limit divorce by parents who are simply bored or unfulfilled. But how should we draw the line between unfulfilling and conflict-ridden marriages? And who should do the drawing?

High-conflict marriages are not necessarily violent or even dramatically quarrelsome like the couple in Edward Albee's *Who's Afraid of Virginia Woolf?* One major recent study operationally defined a high-conflict family as one in which a spouse said the marriage was "not too happy" or the couple had arguments about five out of nine topics, including money, sex, chores, and in-laws. A number of recent studies do show that even moderate levels of marital dissatisfaction can have a detrimental effect on the quality of parenting.

The most critical factor in a child's well-being in any form of family is a close, nurturant relationship with at least one parent. For most children of divorce, this means the mother. Her ability to function as parent is in turn influenced by her physical and psychological well-being. Depression, anger, or stress can make a mother irritable, inconsistent, and in general less able to cope with her children and their problems, whether or not marital difficulties lead to divorce.

Until recently, the typical study of children of divorce began after the separation took place. However, two important studies—one directed by Jack Block and another by Andrew Cherlin—examined data on children long before their parents divorced. These studies found that child problems usually attributed to the divorce could be seen months and even years earlier. Usually, these results are assumed to reflect the impact of family conflict on children. But in a recent book analyzing divorce trends around the world, William J. Goode offers another possibility:

> The research not only shows that many of the so-called effects of divorce were present before the marriage, but suggests an even more radical hypothesis: in at least a sizeable number of families the problems that children generate may create parental conflict and thereby increase the likelihood of divorce.

The Effects of Single Parenthood

The problems of never-married single mothers and their children set off some of today's hottest buttons—sex, gender, race, and welfare. Dan Quayle's attack on Murphy Brown confused the issue. It is true that more single, educated, middle-class women are having children. The rate nearly tripled in the last decade among women in professional or managerial occupations. But despite this increase, only 8 percent of professional-status women are never-married, Murphy Brown mothers. Out-of-wedlock births continue to be far more prevalent among the less educated, the poor, and racial minorities.

Most people take the correlation between single parenthood and poverty as proof of a causal relation between the two. But the story is more complex. In his book *America's Children*, Donald Hernandez of the Census Bureau shows that if we take into account the income of fathers in divorced and unwed families, the increase in single mothers since 1959 probably accounts for only 2 to 4 percentage points of today's childhood poverty rates. As Kristen Luker has pointed out in *Dubious Conceptions: The Controversy Over Teen Pregnancy*, the assumption that early childbearing causes poverty and school dropouts is backward; these conditions are as much cause as effect.

Elijah Anderson, Linda Burton, William Julius Wilson, and other urban sociologists have shown the causal connections linking economic conditions and racial stigma with out-of-wedlock births and the prevalence of single-mother families in the inner cities. Cut off from the rest of society, with little or no hope of stable, family-supporting jobs, young men prove their manhood through an "oppositional culture" based on machismo and sexual prowess. Young women, with little hope of either a husband or economic independence, drift into early sexual relationships, pregnancy, and childbirth.

Middle-class families have also been shaken by economic change. The family restorationists, however, have little to say about the impact of economic forces on families. In her *Atlantic* article, Whitehead mentions—almost as an afterthought—that the loss of good jobs has deprived high school graduates across the country as well as inner-city young people of the ability to support families. "Improving job opportunities for young men," she writes, "would enhance their ability and presumably their willingness to form lasting marriages." Yet these considerations do not affect the main thrust of her arguments supporting Quayle's contention that the poor suffer from a "poverty of values.". . .

Creating a Realistic Vision of Families

The family structure debate raises larger questions about the changes in family, gender, and sexuality in the past three decades—what to think about them, what language to use in talking about them. The language of moral decay will not suffice. Many of the nation's churches and synagogues are rethinking ancient habits and codes to accommodate new conceptions of women's equality and new versions of morality and responsibility in an age of sexual relationships outside of marriage and between partners of the same gender.

The nation as a whole is long overdue for a serious discussion of the upheaval in American family life since the 1960s and how to mitigate its social and personal costs, especially to children. The point of reference should not be the lost family of a mythical past conjured up by our nostalgic yearnings but the more realistic vision offered by the rich body of historical scholarship since the 1970s. From the beginning, American families have been diverse, on-the-go, buffeted by social and economic change. The gap between family values and actual behavior has always been wide.

Such a discussion should also reflect an awareness that the family trends we have experienced over the past three decades are not unique. Every other Western country has

72

experienced similar changes in women's roles and family structure. The trends are rooted in the development of the advanced industrial societies. As Andrew Cherlin puts it, "We can no more keep wives at home or slash the divorce rate than we can shut down our cities and send everyone back to the farm."

However, our response to family change has been unique. No other country has experienced anything like the cultural warfare that has made the family one of the most explosive issues in American society. Most other countries, including our cultural sibling Canada, have adapted pragmatically to change and developed policies in support of working parents, single-parent families, and all families raising children. Teenagers in these countries have fewer abortions and out-of-wedlock births, not because they have less sex, but because sex education and contraceptives are widely available.

Sooner or later, we are going to have to let go of the fantasy that we can restore the family of the 1950s. Given the cultural shocks of the past three decades and the quiet depression we have endured since the mid-1970s, it's little wonder that we have been enveloped by a haze of nostalgia. Yet the family patterns of the 1950s Americans now take as the standard for judging family normality were actually a deviation from long-term trends. Since the nineteenth century, the age at marriage, divorce rate, and women's labor force participation had been rising. In the 1950s however, the age of marriage declined, the divorce rate leveled off, the proportion of the population married reached a new high, and the American birth rate approached that of India. After the 1950s, the long-term historical trends resumed.

Most of us would not want to reverse all the trends that have helped to transform family life—declining mortality rates, rising educational levels for both men and women, reliable contraception, and greater opportunities for women. Barring a major cataclysm, the changes in family life are now too deeply woven into American lives to be reversed by "just say no" campaigns. . . .

The task is to buffer children and families from the effects of these trends. Arguing for systematic economic reform in *Mother Jones*, John Judis writes that between the new economic realities and the kinds of broad measures needed to address them, there is "a yawning gulf of politics and ideology into which even the most well-meaning and intelligently conceived policy can tumble." A similar gulf lies between the new realities of American family life and the policies needed to address them.

Periodical Bibliography

The following articles have been selected to supplement the diverse views presented in this chapter. Addresses are provided for periodicals not indexed in the *Readers' Guide to Periodical Literature*, the *Alternative Press Index*, the *Social Sciences Index*, or the *Index to Legal Periodicals and Books*.

Gary Bauer — "Defending the Family," *American Legion Magazine*, August 1998. Available from PO Box 7068, Indianapolis, IN 46207.

Stephanie Coontz — "Unrealistic Family Myths," *USA Today*, December 1997.

Paul deParrie — "Family Values and Godly Standards," *Life Advocate*, May/June 1997. Available from PO Box 13656, Portland, OR 97213.

Paul Gottfried — "Thinking About Secularisms," *World & I*, July 1999. Available from 3400 New York Ave. NE, Washington, DC 20002.

Edward Luttwak — "Turbo-Charged Capitalism Is the Enemy of Family Values," *New Perspectives Quarterly*, Spring 1995.

Hara Estroff Marano — "A New Focus on Family Values," *Psychology Today*, November/December 1997.

Bunnie Riedel — "Beware of False Prophets," *Christian Social Action*, April 1997. Available from 100 Maryland Ave. NE, Washington, DC 20002.

Adriene Sere — "Reality Check: Inequality and the American Family," *Humanist*, May/June 1996.

Harvey Siegel — "Why Everything Is *Not* Relative," *Free Inquiry*, Fall 1998. Available from PO Box 664, Amherst, NY 14226-0664.

Arlene Skolnick — "Family Values: The Sequel," *American Prospect*, May/June 1997.

Joseph Sobran — "The Christian-Secular Conflict," *New American*, December 21, 1998. Available from PO Box 8040, Appleton, WI 54913.

Judith Stacey — "The Father Fixation: Let's Get Real About American Families," *UTNE Reader*, September/October 1996.

CHAPTER 2

Is America in Moral Decline?

Chapter Preface

A glance at any American newspaper published during the late 1990s is enough to convince anyone that the nation is suffering from a collapse of moral values. Accounts of political sex scandals and corruption, parents murdering their children, and ghastly school massacres paint a picture of a society that is morally dissolute, if not outright evil.

On the other hand, recent statistics compiled by the U.S. National Center for Health report encouraging trends in social values, noting that rates of homicide, divorce, illegitimacy, teenage births, and teenage sex have been steadily decreasing since the mid-1990s.

David Whitman, author of *The Optimism Gap: The I'm OK–They're Not Syndrome and the Myth of American Decline*, offers one explanation for these conflicting indicators of morality. Although Americans may regard society as morally corrupt, he contends, they usually feel their own values are positive. According to Whitman, "When members of the public voice distress about family breakdown they are almost always referring to other people's families. Yet the vast majority of citizens do not have serious moral qualms about themselves or their families. Members of the public repeatedly describe their own families as happy ones with strong ties." In Whitman's opinion, fears about moral decline do not reflect the reality of most Americans' lives.

Gertrude Himmelfarb provides a much different analysis of morality in America. Himmelfarb, author of *The Demoralization of Society: From Victorian Virtues to Modern Values*, argues that "from a longer perspective, even the good news [about American values] may give us pause. The decline or stabilization of some of the indices of social disarray does not begin to bring us back to . . . that now maligned period of the 1950s." For example, she notes, although violent crime is lower than it was in the mid-1990s, it is still almost four times that of the 1950s.

The assessments made by Whitman and Himmelfarb illustrate the complexity of America's moral situation. In the following chapter, authors offer diverse opinions on whether America is experiencing a moral decline.

"There is a coarseness, a callousness, a cynicism, a banality, and a vulgarity to our time."

America Faces a Moral Crisis

William J. Bennett

In the following viewpoint, excerpted from a speech delivered to the Heritage Foundation, William J. Bennett argues that America is experiencing a serious crisis of morals, as evidenced by rising rates of violent crime, illegitimacy, divorce, and teen suicide, and declining standards of education. As deviant behavior has grown more prevalent, he contends, society loses its capacity for shock, disgust, and outrage. Bennett blames America's moral decline on a widespread rejection of religion. He is the codirector of the organization Empower America, and the author of a number of books about morality, including *The Death of Outrage: Bill Clinton and the Assault on American Ideals, The Book of Virtues,* and *The De-Valuing of America: The Fight for Our Culture and Our Children.*

As you read, consider the following questions:
1. How do foreigners perceive America, as described by the author?
2. As cited by Bennett, what does the ongoing teacher survey conclude about America's schools?
3. According to Bennett, what is "spiritual acedia," and what impact does it have on society?

Excerpted from "Getting Used to Decadence," speech given by William J. Bennett, December 7, 1993, in Washington, DC. Reprinted with permission from the author.

A few months ago I had lunch with a friend of mine, a man who has written for a number of political journals and who now lives in Asia. During our conversation the topic turned to America—specifically, America as seen through the eyes of foreigners.

During our conversation, he told me what he had observed during his travels: that while the world still regards the United States as the leading economic and military power on earth, this same world no longer beholds us with the moral respect it once did. When the rest of the world looks at America, he said, they see no longer a "shining city on a hill." Instead, they see a society in decline, with exploding rates of crime and social pathologies. We all know that foreigners often come here in fear—and once they are here, they travel in fear. It is our shame to realize that they have good reason to fear; a record number of them get killed here.

Today, many who come to America believe they are visiting a degraded society. Yes, America still offers plenty of jobs, enormous opportunity, and unmatched material and physical comforts. But there is a growing sense among many foreigners that when they come here, they are slumming. I have, like many of us, an instinctive aversion to foreigners harshly judging my nation; yet I must concede that much of what they think is true.

I recently had a conversation with a D.C. cab driver who is doing graduate work at American University. He told me that once he receives his masters degree he is going back to Africa. His reason? His children. He doesn't think they are safe in Washington. He told me that he didn't want them to grow up in a country where young men will paw his daughter and expect her to be an "easy target," and where his son might be a different kind of target—the target of violence from the hands of other young males. "It is more civilized where I come from," said this man from Africa. I urged him to move outside of Washington; things should improve.

America Through Foreign Eyes

But it is not only violence and urban terror that signal decay. We see it in many forms. *Newsweek* columnist Joe Klein recently wrote about Berenice Belizaire, a young Haitian girl who arrived in New York in 1987. When she arrived in America she spoke no English and her family lived in a cramped Brooklyn apartment. Eventually Berenice enrolled at James Madison High School, where she excelled. According to Judith Khan, a math teacher at James Madison, "[The immigrants are] why I love teaching in Brooklyn. They have a drive in them that we no longer seem to have."

And far from New York City, in the beautiful Berkshire mountains where I went to school, Philip Kasinitz, an assistant professor of sociology at Williams College, has observed that Americans have become the object of ridicule among immigrant students on campus. "There's an interesting phenomenon. When immigrant kids criticize each other for getting lazy or loose, they say, 'You're becoming American,'" Kasinitz says. "Those who work hardest to keep American culture at bay have the best chance of becoming American success stories."

An article published in the *Washington Post* pointed out how students from other countries adapt to the lifestyle of most American teens. Paulina, a Polish high school student studying in the United States, said that when she first came here she was amazed by the way teens spent their time. According to Paulina:

> In Warsaw, we would talk to friends after school, go home and eat with our parents and then do four or five hours of homework. When I first came here, it was like going into a crazy world, but now I am getting used to it. I'm going to Pizza Hut and watching TV and doing less work in school. I can tell it is not a good thing to get used to.

Think long and hard about these words, spoken by a young Polish girl about America: "When I first came here it was like going into a crazy world, but now I am getting used to it." And, "I can tell it is not a good thing to get used to."

Something has gone wrong with us.

This is a conclusion which I come to with great reluctance. During the late 1960s and 1970s, I was one of those who reacted strongly to criticisms of America that swept across university campuses. I believe that many of those criticisms—"Amerika" as an inherently repressive, imperialist, and racist society—were wrong then, and they are wrong now. But intellectual honesty demands that we accept facts that we would sometimes like to wish away. Hard truths are truths nonetheless. And the hard truth is that something has gone wrong with us.

America is not in danger of becoming a third world country; we are too rich, too proud and too strong to allow that to happen. It is not that we live in a society completely devoid of virtue. Many people live well, decently, even honorably. There are families, schools, churches and neighborhoods that work. There are places where virtue is taught and learned. But there is a lot less of this than there ought to be. And we know it. John Updike put it this way: "The fact that . . . we still live well cannot ease the pain of feeling that we no longer live nobly."

Empirical Evidence of Social Regression

Let me briefly outline some of the empirical evidence that points to cultural decline, evidence that while we live well materially, we don't live nobly. Earlier this year I released, through the auspices of the Heritage Foundation, *The Index of Leading Cultural Indicators*, the most comprehensive statistical portrait available of behavioral trends over the last thirty years. Among the findings: since 1960, the population has increased 41 percent; the Gross Domestic Product has nearly tripled; and total social spending by all levels of government (measured in constant 1990 dollars) has risen from $142.73 billion to $787.00 billion—more than a five-fold increase.

But during the same thirty-year period, there has been a 560 percent increase in violent crime; more than a 400 percent increase in illegitimate births; a quadrupling in divorces; a tripling of the percentage of children living in single-parent homes; more than a 200 percent increase in the teenage suicide rate; and a drop of 75 points in the average S.A.T. scores of high-school students.

These are not good things to get used to.

Today 30 percent of all births and 68 percent of black births are illegitimate. By the end of the decade, according to the most reliable projections, 40 percent of all American births and 80 percent of minority births will occur out of wedlock.

These are not good things to get used to.

And then there are the results of an on-going teacher survey. Over the years teachers have been asked to identify the top problems in America's schools. In 1940 teachers identified them as talking out of turn; chewing gum; making noise; running in the hall; cutting in line; dress code infractions; and littering. When asked the same question in1990, teachers identified drug use; alcohol abuse; pregnancy; suicide; rape; robbery; and assault.

These are not good things to get used to, either.

Consider, too, where the United States ranks in comparison with the rest of the industrialized world. We are at or near the top in rates of abortions, divorces, and unwed births. We lead the industrialized world in murder, rape and violent crime. And in elementary and secondary education, we are at or near the bottom in achievement scores.

The American Ethos

These facts alone are evidence of substantial social regression. But there are other signs of decay, ones that do not so easily lend themselves to quantitative analyses (some of which I have already suggested in my opening anecdotes). What I am talking about is the moral, spiritual and aesthetic character and habits of a society—what the ancient Greeks referred to as its ethos. And here, too, we are facing serious problems. For there is a coarseness, a callousness, a cynicism, a banality, and a vulgarity to our time. There are just too many signs of de-civilization—that is, civilization gone rotten. And the worst of it has to do with our children. Apart from the numbers and the specific facts, there is the ongoing, chronic crime against children: the crime of making them old before their time. We live in a culture which at times seems almost dedicated to the corruption of the young, to assuring the loss of their innocence before their time.

This may sound overly pessimistic or even alarmist, but I think this is the way it is. And my worry is that people are not unsettled enough; I don't think we are angry enough. We have become inured to the cultural rot that is setting in. Like Paulina, we are getting used to it, even though it is not a good thing to get used to. People are experiencing atrocity overload, losing their capacity for shock, disgust and out-rage. A few weeks ago eleven people were murdered in New York City within ten hours—and as far as I can tell, it barely caused a stir.

A Diseased Society

The diseases incident to American society are moral and cul-tural rather than political: the collapse of ethical principles and habits, the loss of respect for authorities and institutions, the breakdown of the family, the decline of civility, the vul-garization of high culture, and the degradation of popular culture. Three-quarters of the people in a recent poll said that the main cause of America's problems is "moral decay."

In their most virulent form these diseases manifest them-selves in illegitimacy, crime, violence, drug addiction, illiter-acy, pornography, and welfare dependency. Some of these conditions have improved in recent years, but there is little cause for complacency. If the number of births to teenagers has decreased, the proportion of out-of-wedlock births, to adults as well as teenagers, continues to increase (and this country still has the dubious distinction of having the high-est rate of teenage pregnancy in the industrialized world). If divorce is tapering off, it is because cohabitation is becoming so common; people living together without benefit of mar-riage can separate without benefit of divorce. (And do so with greater facility and frequency.) If there are fewer abor-tions, it is in part because illegitimacy has become more re-spectable. (Indeed, the term "illegitimacy" is taboo; the pre-ferred terms in official circles are "non-marital childbearing" or "alternative mode of parenting.") If one drug falls out of favor, another takes its place; and the decline among adults is more than offset by an increase among young people—and progressively younger people. And in spite of the recent de-crease of crime (which, penologists warn us, may be reversed when today's baby boomers become tomorrow's delin-quents), teenage boys, regardless of race, are still more likely to die from gunshot wounds than from all natural causes combined, and homicide is the second leading cause of death for all young people and the leading cause for young blacks.

Gertrude Himmelfarb, *Public Interest*, Spring 1998.

A violent criminal, who mugged and almost killed a 72-year-old man and was shot by a police officer while fleeing the scene of the crime, was awarded $4.3 million. Virtual silence. And during the 1992 Los Angeles riots, Damian Williams and Henry Watson were filmed pulling an innocent man out of a truck, crushing his skull with a brick, and doing a victory dance over his fallen body. Their lawyers then built a successful legal defense on the proposition that people cannot be held accountable for getting caught up in mob violence. ("They just got caught up in the riot," one juror told the *New York Times*. "I guess maybe they were in the wrong place at the wrong time.") When the trial was over and these men were found not guilty on most counts, the sound you heard throughout the land was relief.

We are "defining deviancy down," in Senator Moynihan's memorable phrase. And in the process we are losing a once-reliable sense of civic and moral outrage.

Listen to this story from former New York City Police Commissioner Raymond Kelly:

> A number of years ago there began to appear, in the windows of automobiles parked on the streets of American cities, signs which read: "No radio." Rather than express outrage, or even annoyance at the possibility of a car break-in, people tried to communicate with the potential thief in conciliatory terms. The translation of "no radio" is: "Please break into someone else's car, there's nothing in mine." These "no radio" signs are flags of urban surrender. They are hand-written capitulations. Instead of "no radio," we need new signs that say "no surrender. "

And what is so striking today is not simply the increased number of violent crimes, but the nature of those crimes. It is no longer "just" murder we see, but murders with a prologue, murders accompanied by acts of unspeakable cruelty and inhumanity. . . .

Who's to blame? Here I would caution conservatives against the tendency to blame liberals for our social disorders. Contemporary liberalism does have a lot for which to answer; many of its doctrines have wrought a lot of damage. Universities, intellectuals, think tanks, and government departments have put a lot of poison into the reservoirs of national discourse. But to simply point the finger of blame at liberals and elites is wrong. The hard fact of the matter is that this was not something done to us; it is also something we have done to ourselves. Liberals may have been peddling from an empty wagon, but we were buying.

Much of what I have said is familiar to many of you. But why is this happening? What is behind all this? Well, again, intelligent arguments have been advanced as to why these things have come to pass. Thoughtful people have pointed to materialism and consumerism; an overly permissive society; the writings of Rousseau, Marx, Freud, Nietzsche; the legacy of the 1960s; and so on. There is truth in almost all of these accounts. Let me give you mine.

Spiritual Acedia

I submit to you that the real crisis of our time is spiritual. Specifically, our problem is what the ancients called acedia. Acedia is the sin of sloth. But acedia, as understood by the saints of old, is not laziness about life's affairs (which is what we normally think sloth to be). Acedia is something else; properly understood, acedia is an aversion to and a negation of spiritual things. Acedia reveals itself as an undue concern for external affairs and worldly things. Acedia is spiritual torpor; an absence of zeal for divine things. And it brings with it, according to the ancients, "a sadness, a sorrow of the world." Acedia manifests itself in man's "joyless, ill-tempered, and self-seeking rejection of the nobility of the children of God." The slothful man hates the spiritual, and he wants to be free of its demands. The old theologians taught that acedia arises from a heart steeped in the worldly and carnal, and from a low esteem of divine things. It eventually leads to a hatred of the good altogether. And with hatred comes more rejection, more ill-temper, sadness, and sorrow.

Spiritual acedia is not a new condition, of course. It is the seventh capital sin. But today it is in ascendance. In coming to this conclusion, I have relied on two literary giants—men born on vastly different continents, the product of two completely different worlds, and shaped by wholly different experiences—yet writers who possess strikingly similar views, and who have had a profound impact on my own thinking. It was an unusual and surprising moment to find their views coincident.

When the late novelist Walker Percy was asked what concerned him most about the future of America, he answered:

Probably the fear of seeing America, with all its great strength and beauty and freedom . . . gradually subside into decay through default and be defeated, not by the Communist movement . . . but from within by weariness, boredom, cynicism, greed and in the end helplessness before its great problems.

And here are the words of the prophetic Aleksandr Solzhenitsyn (echoing his 1978 Harvard commencement address in which he warned of the West's "spiritual exhaustion"):

> In the United States the difficulties are not a Minotour or a dragon—not imprisonment, hard labor, death, government harassment and censorship—but cupidity, boredom, sloppiness, indifference. Not the acts of a mighty all-pervading repressive government but the failure of a listless public to make use of the freedom that is its birthright.

A Corruption of the Heart

What afflicts us, then, is a corruption of the heart, a turning away in the soul. Our aspirations, our affections and our desires are turned toward the wrong things. And only when we turn them toward the right things—toward enduring, noble, spiritual things—will things get better.

Lest I leave the impression of bad news on all fronts, I do want to be clear about the areas where I think we have made enormous gains: material comforts, economic prosperity and the spread of democracy around the world. The American people have achieved a standard of living unimagined 50 years ago. We have seen extraordinary advances in medicine, science and technology. Life expectancy has increased more than 20 years during the last six decades. Opportunity and equality have been extended to those who were once denied them. And of course America prevailed in our "long, twilight struggle" against communism.

Impressive achievements all.

Yet even with all of this, the conventional analysis is still that this nation's major challenges have to do with getting more of the same: achieving greater economic growth, job creation, increased trade, health care, or more federal programs. Some of these things are desirable (greater economic growth and increased trade); some of them are not (more federal programs). But to look to any or all of them as the solution to what ails us is akin to assigning names to images and shadows, it so widely misses the mark.

If we have full employment and growth—if we have cities of gold and alabaster—but our children have not learned how to walk in goodness, justice, and mercy, then the American experiment, no matter how gilded, will have failed.

A Bagman's Paradise

I realize I have laid down strong charges, a tough indictment. Some may question them. But if I am wrong, if my diagnosis is not right, then someone must explain to me this: why do Americans feel so bad when things are economically, militarily and materially so good? Why amidst this prosperity and security are enormous numbers of people—almost 70 percent of the public—saying that we are off track? This paradox is described in the Scottish author John Buchan's work. Writing a half-century ago, he described the "coming of a two garish age, when life would be lived in the glare of neon lamps and the spirit would have no solitude." Here is what Buchan wrote about his nightmare world:

> In such a [nightmare] world everyone would have leisure. But everyone would be restless, for there would be no spiritual discipline in life. . . . It would be a feverish, bustling world, self-satisfied and yet malcontent, and under the mask of a riotous life there would be death at the heart. In the perpetual hurry of life there would be no chance of quiet for the soul. . . . In such a bagman's paradise, where life would be rationalised and padded with every material comfort, there would be little satisfaction for the immortal part of man.

During the last decade of the twentieth century, many have achieved this bagman's paradise. And this is not a good thing to get used to.

In identifying spiritual exhaustion as the central problem, I part company with many. There is a disturbing reluctance in our time to talk seriously about matters spiritual and religious. Why? Perhaps it has to do with the modern sensibility's profound discomfort with the language and the commandments of God. Along with other bad habits, we have gotten used to not talking about the things which matter most—and so, we don't.

One will often hear that religious faith is a private matter that does not belong in the public arena. But this analysis does not hold—at least on some important points. Whatever your faith—or even if you have none at all—it is a fact that when millions of people stop believing in God, or when their belief is so attenuated as to be belief in name only, enormous public consequences follow. And when this is accompanied by an aversion to spiritual language by the political and intellectual class, the public consequences are even greater. How could it be otherwise? In modernity, nothing has been more consequential, or more public in its consequences, than large segments of American society privately turning away from God, or considering Him irrelevant, or declaring Him dead. Dostoyevsky reminded us in *The Brothers Karamazov* that "if God does not exist, everything is permissible." We are now seeing "everything." And much of it is not good to get used to.

"The real threat to [America] is not moral decline. It is what Americans do to their own society in the name of arresting moral decline."

America Does Not Face a Moral Crisis

James A. Morone

In the viewpoint that follows, James A. Morone asserts that fears about America's moral crisis are unfounded. In Morone's view, it is simply untrue that society is devoid of religious sentiment, plagued by random violence, and awash in sexual promiscuity. Those who promote hysteria over American morality would rather condemn lifestyles they view as "corrupt" than develop progressive solutions to the real societal problems of crime and poverty. Morone is a professor of political science at Brown University and the author of *The Democratic Wish: Popular Participation and the Limits of American Government.*

As you read, consider the following questions:
1. What evidence does Morone provide that Americans are religious?
2. According to the author, what would a sensible policy on crime attempt to accomplish?
3. Do Americans live in a "divorce culture," in Morone's view?

Excerpted from "The Corrosive Politics of Virtue," by James A. Morone, *The American Prospect*, vol. 26, May/June 1996. Copyright ©1996 by The American Prospect. Reprinted with the permission of the author and *The American Prospect*.

The most influential men in America met in Boston. The nation, they agreed, faced a terrible moral crisis: rampant substance abuse, sex (even the old taboo against naked breasts seemed to be gone), illegitimacy. Public schools were languishing, the pursuit of profits was appalling, the explosion of lawsuits completely out of hand. Worst of all, parents were doing a terrible job of raising their kids—not enough discipline. "Most of the evils" that afflict our society, reported the conference, stem from "defects as to family government." The gathering published a famous call for moral reform in 1679.

More than 300 years later, the old jeremiad is still doing a brisk business. From every political quarter we hear the same story—moral failures vex the nation. Almost no one in public life demurs. The warnings of spiritual decline sound vaguely plausible. Besides, why oppose calls for more virtuous behavior? . . .

The Preachers

Today, the calls to virtue sound across the full spectrum of American culture. At the highbrow end, academics like James Q. Wilson (*The Moral Sense*) and Gertrude Himmelfarb (*The De-Moralization of Society*) set out, as Wilson puts it, "to help people recover the confidence with which they once spoke about virtue and morality."

Among the middlebrow, the footnotes start to melt away and exhortation takes over. William Bennett, Ben Wattenberg, Amitai Etzioni, and many others have enjoyed success thumping rectitude to general audiences. "SHAME," blares the cover of *Newsweek*. The subtitle tells the story: "Intolerance has gotten a bad rap in recent years, but there should be a way to condemn behavior that's socially destructive."

Finally, down at the other end sits the really big morality market. Fundamentalist and evangelical books (and tapes and videos) offer rousing sermons, exhortations, and warnings. Preachers like Tim and Beverly LaHaye construct a vivid narrative of America that can be summed up by the titles they have published in the past three years: *Faith of our Founding Fathers*, *The Spirit Filled Family*, *A Nation Without a Conscience*, and *What Everyone Should Know About Homosexuality*.

Put aside the differences in tone, sophistication, and packaging, and what you find is a startling convergence in the message. From prestigious academics to fundamentalist preachers, the moralists offer very different audiences a consistent narrative about American politics and culture. It is a story in which good people try to cling to their morals despite an overwhelming, sneering, secular tide.

When "ordinary men and women . . . wish to make moral judgments," writes Wilson, "they must do so privately and in whispers." Himmelfarb wonders "whether the million purchasers of William Bennett's *The Book of Virtues* had to overcome their initial embarrassment in order to utter that word." Once upon a time, the dirty pornographer or the embarrassed condom purchaser skulked about. But with the great revolution of American mores, it is now those who would be good who sneak red-faced while pornography is everywhere and condoms (but not prayers!) are passed around in school. Reading across the literary spectrum, the tone moves from tart irony to raw outrage—much of it directed at the federal government for buying condoms while barring Christ from public schools. But the constant message boils down to this: Our society has abandoned the morals that once guided us.

And there will be hell to pay. The trends, writes Himmelfarb, bode "even worse for the future than for the present." Or, as Reverend LaHaye puts it in *The Battle for the Mind:* "For over seventy-five years, judges, legislators, governors, mayors and presidents have introduced legislation based on [secular humanism] which is destructive of morality and family solidarity. We have arrived at the gates of Sodom and Gomorrah." Recall that God burned Sodom and Gomorrah to cinders in His wrath over the people's iniquity (in fact, it's at Sodom where the Bible first raises the specter of brimstone and fire).

How do we avoid that kind of fate? In *Strength For the Journey,* Jerry Falwell puts it directly: God needs us to "save the nation from inward moral decay."

Still Holier than Most

Has America really developed a secular culture that runs down morality and deprecates religion? No. The charge is popular fiction. Every available measure suggests people in the United States continue to talk about God with a gusto unmatched in the Western world. G.K. Chesterton once described the United States as a nation with the soul of a church. The description remains apt.

According to surveys by the Gallup Organization, 95 percent of Americans profess a faith in God—a number that has scarcely budged in years. (The figure is 76 percent in Britain and 52 percent in Sweden.) Or take the common polling routine that probes for belief in the Ten Commandments. Again, no Western nation beats the United States. Getting back to sex, for example, 87 percent of Americans tell pollsters that adultery is "always wrong" compared to 48 percent in France. More than three-quarters of the population belong to a church, a steady 40 percent say they went this week, and 9 percent claim to go to church "several times a week." Only the last figure, reported by the National Opinion Research Center, has changed much in the past two decades—and it is up 30 percent.

The measures of American faith stretch on and on. More than one in four Americans owns at least five Bibles. The Family Channel is one of the top ten cable channels, the Christian Broadcast Network claims a million viewers a day. The pope sells out whenever he prays in an American stadium. So does Billy Graham. And mobs of weeping men go to Promise Keepers rallies and roar approval to variations of the following: Jesus is Number One and we are on His team and we are going to win. (Check out the glossy *Promise Keepers* magazine next time you are at the supermarket.)

Nobody out there is blushing when they whisper "*Virtues*" to the bookseller. . . .

Moral Troubles

But don't we face an unprecedented moral crisis? No. And constructing our policy problems as moral meltdowns make them far more difficult to address.

Start with violent crime. The most reliable statistics are for murder (which unlike, say, spouse abuse, is tough to hush up). Yes, the murder rate is high. In 1995 it was double the rate of 40 years earlier. Murders in New York City are up more than 500 percent since 1960. While other crimes are more difficult to track precisely, they roughly shadow the homicide rate. And according to some analysts, the rise in random violence, like drive-by shootings (instantly flashed in our faces via television), amplify popular anxiety about public order.

Yet the picture of a predatory class awash in ever more violence is misleading. The murder rate last year was precisely what it was 25 years ago—and down 10 percent from the peak in 1980. The murder rate was higher in 1933 than it was in 1996. (And talking about social pathology, the 1933 rate included 28 lynchings.)

The language of looming crisis and lost control are all long-standing features of urban life. Fear of the dangerous classes marked each stage in the evolution of the urban political economy. Abraham Lincoln warned in 1838 of the "outrages committed by mobs" and "the increasing disregard for law which pervades the country." A half century later, Dewitt Talmage, a celebrated nineteenth-century preacher, put it this way, "Boys and girls will play in the streets . . . without police protection" only when Christians take up arms against "the sins of the city." Crime waves, crime panics, and cries for our lost morals are as old as the cities.

Instead of sermonizing and demonizing, a sensible policy would focus on both punishing criminals and addressing the causes of crime—"tough on crime, tough on the causes of crime," as British Labor leader Tony Blair puts it. Perhaps some liberals and progressives were queasy about punishment in the past. But most now recognize that crime makes life in poor neighborhoods especially difficult. That, after all, is where most of the victims live. In *Labor of Love, Labor of Sorrow*, Jacqueline Jones quotes one black woman on raising her family in Washington, D.C., during the 1920s: "I have lived here long enough to know that you can't grow a good potato out of bad ground. This sure is bad ground."

A sensible crime policy also has to address a vast array of underlying causes that run a wide policy spectrum. First, there is the sheer firepower available in America: lots of guns, faster guns, more powerful guns. Almost three million handguns were manufactured and marketed in the U.S. in

1993. Second, it is time for a sustained, national reevaluation of the war on drugs. Our public policies have succeeded in making them scarcer, more expensive, and ironically more lucrative (though wealth is an illusion for most of the young men in the drug business). Third, we face the still more difficult problem of declining demand for unskilled labor. Job growth has always been cyclical, but the postindustrial economy wipes out a major traditional track out of poverty. (And as articles in this magazine have repeatedly demonstrated, the Federal Reserve's crusade against inflation successfully chokes off job growth before employers are reduced to calling on the long-term unemployed.)

The features of an enlightened crime policy stretch on—better education, job training, urban infrastructure, a decent minimum wage. In the long run, these are the kinds of reforms that create a safer and more just society. But the moralizers' message—the resurrection of the dangerous, depraved, urban them—pushes these possibilities right off the policy agenda.

The State of Sexual Morality

Well, what about sex? The preachers positively wallow in their denunciations of the pelvic sins—and here the academics gnash their teeth as loudly as the fundamentalists. The jeremiads all begin with the same premise: We are reaping the bitter harvest of the permissive 1960s culture. But the moralizers disagree on the consequences. Reading from political right to left, we get denunciation of homosexuality, abortion, promiscuity, illegitimacy, teen pregnancy, the collapse of marriage, and kids without dads.

Amid these hot-button issues, one theme gathers broad support: traditional families. Alarm is spreading about the growing number of children being raised by a single parent. The 1990 census puts the figure at 28 percent of all children and 60.6 percent of African American children, up from 21.5 percent and 51.9 percent respectively in 1980. Even sensible moderates gulp hard at those numbers. Surely, concludes the conventional wisdom, this is a genuine moral crisis. Or is it?

Today, divorce is the largest factor, accounting for 40 percent of all the single-parent households in 1990. We live in

a "divorce culture," writes David Blankenhorn in his widely cited book *Fatherless America*. Marriage, according to Blankenhorn, has become "old fashioned, beleaguered, even quaint—a way of life primarily suitable for older or boring people." Somehow, we have got to seize our norms and restore the old marriage culture. But according to the 1990 census, more than 79 percent of the households include a married couple, down undramatically from 82.5 percent a decade earlier. Divorce culture? Hardly.

On a Moral Upswing

There is surprisingly little evidence that Americans act more immorally today than they did a quarter-century ago. In fact, just the opposite seems to be true. . . .

Compared with their predecessors of a quarter-century ago, Americans today are less likely to drink to excess, take drugs, rely on the dole, drive drunk, or knowingly evade paying taxes. They give more money to charity and spend as much or more time in church. And they are more likely than their predecessors to do good Samaritan work among the poor, sick, and elderly. Despite fears of random violence, FBI reports suggest that fewer people were murdered by strangers in 1997 (2,067) than in 1977 (about 2,500), even though the U.S. population grew by 47 million during that time. The dramatic drop in the number of Americans victimized by murder, burglary, and theft represents another well-known illustration of moral progress, but there are many more.

David Whitman, *New Republic*, February 22, 1999.

Yet look at the familiar political result. Once again a large, righteous, properly married audience is primed to tsk at (and regulate) the immoral minority that threatens the social order with its promiscuous behavior. Michigan Governor John Engler has gotten the policy crusade rolling with a proposed law that makes divorce more difficult. Supporters of such laws rest their case on a simple maxim: Divorce is bad for kids.

Of course, not all marriages work and not all families are good for children. The new proposals dust off the old divorce loopholes—alcohol, drugs, cheating, physical abuse, mental abuse. Count on prolonged arguments about what exactly constitutes mental cruelty these days. Defining men-

tal abuse points to the buried question that lies at the very heart of the issue: What is a proper family? What is the social institution we are trying to revive?

Diverse Views on Family

Beneath the clamor for getting both parents under the same roof lies the agitated matter of how the family ought to be organized. Consider the range of strongly felt contemporary views. On the one side, conservative Christians insist that "a woman's call to be a wife and mother is the highest calling." Reverend Jerry Falwell spells out the implicit organizational chart. God intends "the husband . . . to be the decision maker. . . . Wives and children want to follow." For some conservatives, men who cook dinner or women who pursue careers are violating divinely ordained gender roles. Across the cultural spectrum, the organizing statement of the National Organization of Women offers a different perspective: "A true partnership between the sexes demands a different concept of marriage, an equitable sharing of responsibilities of home and children and economic burdens." And still further along on the American cultural spectrum, Heather has two moms.

What has happened is a lot more complex than the images of rampant promiscuity imply. Rather, we have lost our consensus about the nature of the family—or, more precisely, about the nature of the women's role. Nor is this a bad thing. The halcyon days of stable marriage featured dependent women without significant career options or the real prospect of supporting themselves. It is far easier to bar the marriage door when one member of the couple is subordinate and dependent, without any meaningful exit option.

This does not mean giving up. By all means, let us find ways that encourage stable marriages and strong parenting. Change the tax laws. Strengthen the support services that help parents. Mend our communities. But remember that the forces moralizing for marital commitment strongly disagree about what a good marriage is. And the golden era they recall was structured on an inequity that is, happily, fading.

Moreover, trying to lock people into marriage without addressing the root causes of marital breakup is likely to undermine the institution itself—more couples delaying marriage,

declining marriage, and departing marriage without a formal divorce. Ironically, it is apt to push the rest of society toward the patterns that dominate the African American community: mothers who never got married in the first place.

Stereotypes About Out-of-Wedlock Births

Turning to black families switches the focus from divorce to out-of-wedlock births. Fifty-one percent of one-parent black families are headed by moms who never married. Only 21 percent are divorced, compared to 28 percent never-married and 40 percent divorced across all races. The obvious question is why? The obvious answers are wrong.

The stereotype pictures a soaring rate of children bearing children encouraged by overly generous welfare handouts. But there is scant evidence that welfare benefits explain many sins: States with low benefits do not have appreciably lower rates of separation, divorce, or out-of-wedlock births. More important, pregnancy and birth rates among young black teenagers have actually declined. The pregnancy rates fell 13 percent for African American women between 15 and 17 years old in the two decades following 1970. Ironically, condemnation has been shrillest while teen pregnancy rates have declined.

Nor should we idealize past purity. In her Pulitzer Prize-winning *A Midwife's Tale*, Laurel Thatcher Ulrich computed the percentage of first births conceived out of wedlock in and around Hallowell, Maine, between 1785 and 1812. The result was a myth-popping 38 percent.

Still, out-of-wedlock births are high and growing as a proportion of all births among African Americans (in part because births among married women have declined). More careful recent analyses point to a series of structural causes of the rise in out-of-wedlock births: the great migration to the urban north; the lack of "marriageable males" in the black community (according to William Julius Wilson, there are 84 black men for every 100 women in the black community, compared to 99 per 100 among whites); and the relatively greater economic power black women have in their relations with black men (partially because of high unemployment among black males).

A Struggle for Meaning and Dignity

However, even sophisticated analyses often overlook the women themselves. As Adolf Reed commented in a review of William Julius Wilson's *The Truly Disadvantaged*, women in the inner city have devised a "network of organizational and institutional forms" that "create meaning and dignity in lives bitterly constrained by forces apparently beyond their control." Their marriage and childbearing choices are part of that struggle for meaning and dignity. This is not to say that these decisions are always ideal, but neither hectoring them with sermons nor using public policy to punish them is likely to create strong two-parent families.

What about the kids? Precisely the right question. How do we improve the lives of American children? The real answers involve sustained commitment to improving education, health care, housing, and child care; training and decent wages for parents; jobs and institutional infrastructure for communities. As a society, we went a long way to improving the life chances of our children's grandparents—the poverty rates among the elderly have declined dramatically in the past generation. The question is how to do the same for children. Addressing that question may go a long way to solving the dilemma of single parents.

The chances of succeeding at any of this are not improved one whit by the morality project. On the contrary, we will not mend our imaginary community nor restore a more generous, universalistic public spirit until we put aside the images of an immoral, unvirtuous them.

The Contemporary Morality Project

Contemporary moralizing lays the burden for American troubles squarely on the shoulders of troublesome Americans. There is an alternative to this emphasis on corrupt individuals.

Throughout American history, religion has inspired reformers to fight against legal and economic injustice—to fight for individuals. Moral crusades rouse Americans to expand rights, overcome biases, attack inequity.

The paradigmatic cases are familiar: abolitionism after 1830, the women's movement in the second half of the nineteenth century, the civil rights movement of the twentieth century. Each invoked a higher morality to challenge exclusion and injustice. But perhaps this different kind of moral crusade is most clearly illustrated by a less familiar case.

At the end of the nineteenth century, the social gospel movement self-consciously emphasized the moral responsibilities of the powerful toward the poor. Those who profited from the new economic order were accountable for the burdens it placed on their workers. As Walter Rauschenbusch, the best-known author of the movement, put it: "During the great industrial crisis in the '90s, I . . . could hear virtue crackling and crumbling all around. If anyone has a sound reason for taking the competitive system by the throat in righteous wrath, it is the unmarried woman and the mother with girls." Drawing on religious imagery and language, Rauschenbusch scorched the inhumanity of "our industrial machine" for the moral pressures that it put on good men and women.

Charles Sheldon's *In His Steps*, an extraordinarily popular novel of the same period, pictured how a midwestern town (Topeka, Kansas) would change if all its leaders were guided by the simple question, "What would Jesus do?" There is plenty of silliness throughout the book. But Sheldon imagines the business leaders of the Gilded Age getting religion and running out to meet their workers—to shake their hands and listen to them with respect.

A Lack of Social Vision

The sinking feeling one gets trekking across the tomes and the tapes of the contemporary morality project comes from the complete absence of even this (rather feeble) social vision. The poor ought to learn to give back to society—more church and less crime, more discipline and fewer delinquents. But rarely a word of how the society and its rules might be biased. Not a hint of going out and listening to the workers with respect—much less helping them struggle with the dislocations of economic transformation.

Despite the thunder, American spiritual life is not going to hell. What all that moralizing does is to organize American rhetoric against social justice, against progressive politics, against national community altogether. In an era when many poor Americans struggle extraordinarily hard, the preachers blame them for their own poverty, turn them on one another, turn Americans against themselves.

The story of moral depravity is well worn. Americans have survived their own unprecedented wickedness—many times. The moralizing routine was already old when the Synod of 1679 published its list of sins. The real threat is not moral decline. It is what Americans do to their own society in the name of arresting moral decline.

| *"Popular culture has become almost uniformly vulgar."*

Popular Culture Is in Decline

Herbert I. London

Herbert I. London charges in the subsequent viewpoint that American popular culture is characterized by a perverse obsession with celebrity. London contends that society grants celebrity status to people who engage in abhorrent behavior, and lavishes these celebrities with media attention while ignoring events of world significance. The American fascination with the vulgar and scandalous has created a culture that exalts obscene language, sexual lasciviousness, and lurid representations of violence, he claims. London is a professor of humanities at New York University and the publisher of *American Outlook* magazine. He is the author of a number of books, including *From the Empire State to the Vampire State: New York in a Downward Transition*.

As you read, consider the following questions:
1. What is the difference between "fame" and "infamy," as stated by the author?
2. What should be the basis of celebrity status, in London's opinion?
3. What examples does London provide to support his claim that the United States values sensual pleasures above all else?

Excerpted from "Outrage, Infamy, and the Celebrity Cult," by Herbert I. London, *American Outlook*, Fall 1998. Reprinted with permission from the author.

While there are many visible manifestations of a national cultural slide in the United States, with ethical relativism and multiculturalism at the forefront, three conditions seem to embody this state of affairs most clearly: an emphasis on celebrity journalism, an inability to elicit public outrage, and the societal confusion between fame and infamy.

At this time when words mean whatever you want them to mean, when Orwellian logic intrudes on every dimension of public life, and when self-styled postmodernists deconstruct texts as if they were used tissues, there are very few surprises that can emerge from the misuse of language. Two words, however, have become so entangled in the popular imagination that they are quintessential examples of the present linguistic—and moral—confusion.

Some time ago—one cannot discern precisely when the balance tilted—infamy and fame had clear, discernible meanings. *Infamy* clearly designated a reputation derived from an evil, brutal, or criminal act, and *fame* was related to positive public estimation. The current edition of Webster's Collegiate Dictionary uses *renown* as a synonym for *fame*. But one could easily apply words such as *celebrated*, *eminent*, *distinguished*, and *illustrious* as well. In short, *infamous* and *famous* were opposite poles separated by a divide of social deeds, those approved and those disavowed.

Recognition as the Standard for Fame

Today, however, attention or recognition is the main standard by which celebrities are judged, and any act that draws newsprint or television space, however questionable, attains considerable acceptability. Engaging in the bizarre has great benefits if in the end it enhances one's celebrity status. Hence the comedienne Whoopi Goldberg is admired for her irreverence, even though it takes the form of using obscenities (or perhaps precisely because it does). Basketball player Dennis Rodman has become a national figure, despite his one-dimensional basketball talent, because he dyes his hair a variety of unattractive colors, adorns his body with tattoos, sometimes wears lipstick and eye makeup, and wore a wedding dress to a book signing. Richard Morris, formerly an advisor to President Clinton, was discovered to have had regular liaisons with a prostitute whom he allowed to listen in on his telephone conversations with the president. For this indiscretion and others he was rewarded with a seven-figure book contract, a newspaper column, and pundit status on television.

What is going on here is that as standards for public approbation have dissolved like soap bubbles, only recognition counts. It is less important that a celebrity be admired than that he or she simply be recognized. As a consequence, a popular figure like Madonna who has limited singing range and even more limited acting ability is universally admired for her ability to market herself as a celebrity. Never mind that this marketing takes the form of public nudity, blasphemy, depicting herself in degrading sexual acts, and the rest of her unique brand of immorality. She is, as they say in the business, recognizable, and that means marketable.

When television sitcom actress Ellen DeGeneres "came out of the closet," her show's ratings skyrocketed (temporarily). Until that point her program had been slated for cancellation.

It is therefore somewhat understandable that infamy and fame have become indistinguishable. Marketing undergirds the manufacture of celebrities, and getting people to notice you is all that counts, so handlers push the envelope of attention, forcing the culture to new extremes. What was *avant-garde* yesterday is *passé* today. Recently a young man who engaged in a brutal murder said, unrepentantly, "Well, at least now I'll be noticed." Alas, he was correct.

Television news exalts the bizarre by bringing to the screen every perversity the mind can conjure. Even guilt is fast becoming an anachronism in an era when recognition is on center stage. Many rock musicians revel in shocking their audiences while insisting that the cameras remain trained on them. The willingness of public figures to act in a dignified manner or be self-effacing is increasingly undermined by the demands of public relations flacks and a sensation-hungry populace.

Truth in Cultural Labeling

These practices are likely to continue unabated as long as aberrant behavior continues to bring significant rewards, but it might help at the margin if we started to label behavior accurately. Fame and infamy should be disentangled. The good should not be confused with the bad. When perversity brings rewards through celebrity, we should describe this as infamy. When people derive celebrity status from acts of genuine charity, concern for others, and behavior that should be emulated, we should call them famous—and only then.

Fame must be reserved for those whose behavior is praiseworthy, and must be denied to the desecraters of culture. Tupac Shakur was infamous, not famous. Donald Trump is infamous, not famous. Don King is infamous, not famous. It may be in the interest of the *National Enquirer* or *Star* magazine to confuse these words, but to those of us who realize that civilization rests on a gossamer-thin foundation of norms and traditions, it is clear that such tears at the fabric of society are not easily repaired. Those who heal our social wounds deserve fame; those who inflict those wounds deserve infamy.

Hunter. Copyright ©1997 News World Communications, Inc. Reprinted by permission of *The Washington Times*.

There was a time not so long ago when the pictures on the front page of the *New York Times* or *Washington Post* were of popes, presidents, and other influential leaders. Celebrities of the movie-star variety or from the publishing world were restricted to the back pages, where one was accustomed to reading about their latest exploits only after perusing more important stories. That condition has now changed.

When the editors of the *New York Times* place Tina Brown's picture on the front page accompanying a story of her resignation as editor of the *New Yorker* magazine, and many other papers follow suit, the era of celebrity journalism is clearly in its ascendancy. After all, Ms. Brown, whatever her talents, is certainly not a world leader; one might even regard her influence as narrowly circumscribed within the magazine industry, a very small slice of the domestic economy. How, then, does she qualify for a front-page photo?

The answer is more obvious than it might have been twenty years ago. We live in a celebrity age. What is deemed important now may be related more to connections and media hype than any objective reality. Ms. Brown is a creation of her own carefully manipulated personal and professional relationships.

Of course, she is far from alone. Millions of dollars are being spent to promote personalities. In the past, newspaper editors could distinguish between promotion and accomplishment. That distinction, however, is increasingly being blurred by bad judgment, television notoriety, and the tabloidization of serious newspapers. It sometimes appears that the major newspapers simply put in small print what the tabloids splash out in bold letters. Other than that, much of the content is quite similar.

Culture is king at the moment, forcing decisions that would have embarrassed editors of yesteryear. Clearly Frank Sinatra was an important cultural icon, but did news of his death belong on the front page? The judgment being made here is that celebrity status itself is newsworthy. Thus celebrity begets more celebrity, and judgment is set aside altogether.

Bad Journalism Driving Out the Good

One might well ask whether in the post-Cold War period vapid cultural stories have driven serious journalism out of existence altogether or, at the least, off the front page. Perhaps the lack of a clear and present international danger has combined with a relatively robust economy to induce a complacency that makes all stories seem equally inconsequential. That would go a long way toward explaining the increased interest in politicians' personal lives. Surely popular culture and highbrow culture are now one and the same, defying distinctions that were once taken for granted and, in my judgment, should still be.

Is Dennis Rodman, for example, a basketball player for the Chicago Bulls, the author of an autobiography of decidedly questionable taste, a freak of nature, or the public relations director for Dennis Rodman Enterprises? Moreover, if Rodman were to do something even more outrageous than his present practices, such as marrying a princess from Monaco while wearing a wedding gown, would that merit a front-page story? One can hardly doubt that it would receive the same coverage previously reserved for notable public events.

The nation is caught up in the celebrity trap. People who appear on television are *ipso facto* stars worthy of national attention. When Jerry Seinfeld brought his television program to an end, the nation shed tears of remorse and editors devoted front-page stories to the occasion even though it had been anticipated for months. One might think that something truly terrible had occurred.

Most significantly, the truly important issues are thus relegated to the back pages. Whatever happened to the story about the Loral Corporation and its sale of a missile-guidance system to the Chinese military? What is the current state of so-called peace negotiations in the Middle East? Is the Asian banking crisis affecting the earnings of American corporations? And what are the implications of all these events for our future peace and prosperity?

There is so much I would like to know. Instead, I am told that Tina Brown is moving from the *New Yorker* to take a job for Disney's Miramax film subsidiary, editing a magazine explicitly designed to provide PR for the company's films. Should I really care? Only insofar as it shows a further decline in the independence of journalists from the people they cover.

Current journalistic practice seems to appeal to the superficial and banal. Here today, gone tomorrow. It is as if Andy Warhol were selecting the personalities now routinely profiled on the front pages of formerly serious newspapers.

I do not expect to see any changes soon. After all, television programming influences every dimension of our lives. And what you see on television becomes reality even when misleading or utterly bogus. That, apparently, has become true for print journalism as well.

"Tell it like it is" is a cliché employed by people who never tell it like it is. Once-serious newspapers, purportedly presenting all the news that is fit to print, now publish little more than the news that celebrity hounds want to read, and it becomes increasingly difficult to distinguish them from papers of the explicitly disposable variety sold at supermarket checkout lines.

Culture in Decline

In the 1930s, Pitirim Sorokin, in his book *Crisis of the Age*, argued that the West had entered into an "advanced sensate age," a period in which sensual pleasures are superordinated over other values such as the idealistic or ideational. That was more than fifty years ago. One can only wonder what Sorokin would say about that same culture today, a milieu that has been so degraded and polluted and is so widely disseminated that the average person unknowingly acquiesces in his own degradation.

If this notion seems exaggerated, consider the following situation. As a result of alleged presidential misbehavior, oral sex is a topic for daily news programming. Kathleen Willey, one of the women accusing President Clinton of sexual misconduct, said on national television that the president forced her to touch his genitals. The Independent Counsel's Report on the president provides revelations of X-rated activities in the White House that are far from family reading. Concerned parents routinely hit their television's "mute" button when a news story on the president comes on.

In Jonesboro, Arkansas, two boys aged eleven and thirteen shot and killed four girls and a teacher because—as several reports noted—a girlfriend broke up with the elder of the two. And in Colorado, a murdered six-year-old girl was revealed to have been a regular participant in a bizarre world of childhood fashion shows. This juicy element engendered a level of national news coverage previously unheard of in such cases, however tragic the incident may have been.

The tragic is now trumped by the tawdry.

Deeper into the Muck

Evidence provided by television researchers suggests that network shows are becoming racier to attract larger audiences. A recent study by the Parents' Television Council found that vulgar language on television programming had increased by 4 percent on a per-hour basis in two years. This nastiness also pervades the plots. On the season finale of *Dharma and Greg*, for instance, the stars engaged in sexual activity in public places. This tasteless story line occurred in an alleged comedy airing at 8:30 p.m.—7:30 in the more socially conservative states in the Central time zone—even though the program was obviously unsuitable viewing for any family other than the Borgias.

Raunchiness is the crux of almost all successful rap music. In fact, after the leading rap group N.W.A.'s approbation of rape, violence, and general mayhem there is little that remains for the imagination of even the most perverse listener. MTV cheerfully explores the boundaries of acceptable viewing, with partial nudity and simulated scenes of fornication now the norm.

In the recent film *The Wedding Singer*, one of the female characters, employing crude language once reserved for sailors on furlough, tells the lead actor that if he enters her home, bedroom delights await him. That is hardly an unusual scene in films today, but what is particularly dismaying is that major newspapers described this film as "sweet and uplifting."

Teen magazines that once restricted copy to the latest fashions and what kids were reading now emphasize the loss of virginity and how to achieve orgasm.

Riding on a public conveyance in any American city will quickly confirm that civility has been interred. Young people almost never give elderly people a seat, and people rarely cover their mouths when coughing.

The language heard on the streets is yet another symptom of degradation. Even middle-class children employ the "f" word as an adjective for any activity, whether pleasant or unpleasant. Of course, the models for this contamination of language can be found in pseudo-sophisticated adults such as those in Joe Klein's roman à clef, *Primary Colors*, and movies like the Julia Roberts comedy *My Best Friend's Wedding*, where the continual use of obscenities is presented as a sign of toughness and sophistication.

At the 1998 Academy Awards ceremony, Ben Affleck, receiving an Oscar for the screenplay of *Good Will Hunting*, told a billion viewers, "I thought this night would either suck or be great." This from a person winning an award for best screenplay!

It was recently reported that at least 65 percent of American students cheat on exams and see nothing wrong with it.

In high-powered college basketball and football programs it is not uncommon for star players to be indicted for rape, assault, robbery, and other felony offenses. Fresno State University basketball coach Jerry "Tark" Tarkanian rationalized the criminal records of some of his players by noting, "Someone has to give them a chance." One might well be forgiven for doubting that Tark would give these young jocks a chance if they couldn't hit a three-point shot or dunk a basketball.

The local news on major stations is invariably a litany of lurid murders and rapes with the most grisly details graphically elaborated. Such nightmarish scenes comprise the pre-sleep fare for millions of Americans.

In her recent decision to throw out the Paula Jones suit against the president, Judge Susan Webber Wright argued that the allegations against Mr. Clinton had not merited the complainant's "claim of outrage." What was the assertion that she judged so trivial? That then-governor Clinton dropped his pants in Paula Jones's presence and, when she refused his "advances," warned her to keep quiet about it.

Uniform Vulgarity

Further examples abound. Each week brings new illustrations of perversity and cultural degradation. Nonetheless, and quite curiously, many analysts of the cultural scene, both liberal and conservative, refer to the common sense of the American public. One might expect moral decay of this magnitude to lead to a public outcry of "Stop this merry-go-round—I want to get off." But such concern is not now evident.

I would contend that the average person has been desensitized; most of our neighbors can no longer distinguish between worthwhile pursuits and cultural detritus. Television programming is not the sole villain, but it is a leader of the pack. Incrementally, it pushes the normative umbrella to new and untested limits as producers gamble that cruder programming will separate their wares from the crowd and engender viewers' interest when the last round of shocking programs seems no longer quite so provocative.

For producers of any popular cultural vehicle there is only one test that counts: audience share. Taste always seems to take a back seat to popularity—or perhaps we had best call it notoriety—and ratings and the V-chip merely provide the cover for ever more irresponsible programming.

Programmers know that the effect of culture is osmotic; there is no way that any parent can effectively insulate his children from the vulgar and titillating nonsense that surrounds us. Popular culture has become almost uniformly vulgar, and we have slid down a moral trap door, as Sorokin predicted. We are beyond outrage, indeed beyond the sensate. We are a people changed without our knowledge or choice.

Perhaps we are already beyond hope, although the seeds of cultural regeneration may reside in the very muck of popular culture. If its blatant indecency should drive audiences to more edifying fare, a scenario of regeneration is possible. What remains to be seen is whether these seeds, if they do exist, will receive enough nourishment to thrive and regenerate our arid cultural landscape. Until the society recovers its ability to distinguish between fame and infamy, between the worthwhile and the banal, between the uplifting and the degrading, such a renaissance seems unlikely.

|"Contemporary Western culture, especially in the United States, is flourishing."

Popular Culture Is Not in Decline

Tyler Cowen

The notion that American culture is experiencing corruption and decline is false, argues Tyler Cowen in the following viewpoint. In truth, Cowen maintains, Western culture has been steadily improving for the past thousand years. The many impressive creations of contemporary culture, he contends, include cinema, rock 'n roll, pop art, jazz, and a brand-new artistic medium: the World Wide Web. Technological and economic progress hold great potential for further cultural innovation, Cowen writes, and those who are pessimistic about popular culture merely fear change. Cowen, a professor of economics at George Mason University, is the author of the book *In Praise of Commercial Culture*.

As you read, consider the following questions:
1. What does Cowen assert about the state of literacy and reading in America?
2. How are new or newly deregulated technologies likely to induce further cultural innovation, in Cowen's view?
3. What reasons does the author provide for why cultural pessimism has flourished?

Excerpted from "Is Our Culture in Decline?" by Tyler Cowen, *Cato Policy Report*, September/October 1998. Reprinted with the permission of the Cato Institute.

The "culture wars". . . reflect deep disagreements about the health of contemporary culture. The current wave of cultural pessimism, expressed in various forms by both the left and the right, suggests that our culture is experiencing corruption and decline. The left concludes that government support for the arts is needed, while the right often favors government support for traditional culture. But a review of the evidence offers strong reasons for cultural optimism and confidence that a modern commercial society will stimulate artistic creativity and diversity.

The music of Bach, Mozart, Haydn, and Beethoven is more accessible to today's listeners than it was to the listeners of the 18th or 19th centuries. Modern concertgoers can sample an unparalleled range of musical periods, instruments, and styles. Even relatively obscure composers have their material stocked in music superstores, which are common in both American cities and suburbs. A small Tower Records outlet will offer at least 10,000 classical music titles, and the largest Tower branch in Manhattan has over 22,000 titles. The Naxos label markets excellent performances of the classics for as little as $5.99 for 70 minutes of music. Music of all kinds—both old and new—is available in great profusion.

Movies, including many silents, can be rented on videocassette very cheaply, or on laser disks for those who want higher quality picture and sound. Modern video stores, run on a private for-profit basis, are libraries full of classic works.

New and definitive editions of many literary works, or better translations, are published regularly. The Bible and Plato, two favorites of many cultural pessimists, continue to be reissued in new editions, while the classics are available in cheap paperback. Television, video stores, and bookstores give modern fans better access to the works of Shakespeare than the Elizabethans had.

Literacy and reading are two areas where the modern world comes in for especially harsh criticism, but even here the trends are largely positive. Between 1970 and 1990 the measured world literacy rate for adults rose from 61.5 to 73.5 percent. The industrialized countries increased their literacy rate from 93.8 to 96.7 percent over that period. American illiteracy was far worse 100 years ago or even in the middle of this century. Consistent with those trends, the average American buys more than twice as many books today as in 1947. The number of bookstores has jumped nearly 10-fold, and their average size has increased dramatically. Book superstores are now commonplace.

Contrary to many claims, television and the Internet are not killing the book. The printed word offers unique modes of storytelling and analysis that other media have not replaced. Television and the Internet often complement reading and stimulate reader interest in books, instead of replacing them. Today a wide variety of talented writers is actively publishing and transcending traditional genre boundaries.

Art museums and art museum attendance are booming. Blockbuster art exhibitions travel the world and bring great paintings to increasing numbers of viewers. Earlier in this century, most Americans outside New York had few means of viewing high-quality art. Art publishing is doing well; even minor painters now have published catalogs full of high-quality color plates.

Live performance of the arts has flourished as well. From 1965 to 1990 America grew from having 58 symphony orchestras to having nearly 300, from 27 opera companies to more than 150, and from 22 nonprofit regional theaters to 500. Contemporary Western culture, especially in the United States, is flourishing.

Markets Spur Innovation

The market economy continually spurs new artistic innovations. Arguing the worth of particular contemporary creations is more difficult, given the tendencies for disagreement about the culture of the present day (Mozart was controversial in his time, but few dispute his merits today). Modern creators, however, have offered many deep and lasting creations, which are universal in their scope and significant in their import. Those creations delight and enrich large numbers of intelligent fans and influence subsequent artists. We can fully expect many modern and contemporary works to stand the test of time, just as earlier works have, even if we cannot identify exactly which ones.

The most impressive creations of contemporary culture

include cinema, rock 'n' roll, Pop Art and Minimalism, modern dance, jazz, genre fiction, and the modern biography, to give but a few examples. The skylines of Manhattan, Chicago, and Hong Kong were financed and designed almost entirely by the private sector. The exact contents of a list of important contemporary creations will vary with taste, but our culture provides a wide variety of styles, aesthetics, and moods. An individual need not have a very particular set of preferences to love contemporary creations. The 20th century is not only the age of intellectual, atonal music, it is also the age of Buddy Holly and Steven Spielberg, both life-affirming and celebratory creators.

New musical genres continue to blossom. Our century has seen the development of blues, soul, rhythm and blues, jazz, ragtime, swing, rock, country and western, rap, and bluegrass, as well as more recent forms of electronic music. Some of the most significant modern artists are still around, playing and recording for our enjoyment. We can hear Bob Dylan and the Rolling Stones in concert, still in good form, even if not at their youthful peak.

Film is the art of the 20th century, par excellence. It combines drama, music, and high technology to entertain and inspire large audiences. Moviegoers all around the world want to see American films. Some movie buffs complain that "they don't make 'em like they used to," but the best American films of the last 20 years—my list would include *The Thin Blue Line, Blue Velvet, Basic Instinct, Schindler's List, Dangerous Liaisons, L.A. Confidential, Titanic,* and *The Truman Show*—belie that opinion. (The viewer who disagrees with my list will have no trouble coming up with his or her own favorites.) Art movies and independent films show continued vitality.

Technology's Cultural Potential

New or newly deregulated technologies are likely to induce further cultural innovations. Cable television is expanding rapidly and breaking down the hegemony of the networks. Eventually viewers will be able to choose from hundreds of channels. Cable already offers the world's greatest movies; the modem drama of sporting events; large doses of popular music; and high arts such as ballet, theater, and classical music. Viewers can take a class in Shakespeare without leaving their living rooms or use foreign-language channels to learn languages, thereby enlarging their access to the world's cultural treasures.

Cable is not the only new artistic medium. We can only guess at the development of the Web, Virtual Reality technologies, and Hypertext, both as means for delivering older creations and as new media for future works.

Finally, quasi-artistic activities are blossoming like never before. Fashion, decoration, cuisine, sports, product design, computer graphics, and commercial art—to give just a few examples—continue to flourish and grow. As recently as 20 years ago, Thai food was not available in most American cities; now Thai restaurants dot the suburbs as well. Although those fields are not art in the narrow sense, they bring beauty and drama into our lives. A beautifully decorated home or a luxurious shopping mall delights us and appeals to our aesthetic sense. The question "What is art?" has become less meaningful with the growing diversity of capitalist production. . . .

Cultural Pessimism and Its Appeal

Western culture has been on an upswing since at least the year 1000. Both innovation and preservation of the past have blossomed. Why then has cultural pessimism had so much influence?

Cognitive biases induce observers to grant cultural pessimism more plausibility than it deserves. The pessimists focus on the decline of what they already appreciate, and neglect the rise of what is yet to come. It is easy to perceive the loss of what we know and harder to discern new developments and surprises. Even if long-term trends are positive, culture may appear to be deteriorating.

Observers often judge present culture against the very best of past culture, causing the present to appear lacking in contrast. But comparing the best of the past against the entirety of the present is unfair. No matter how vital contemporary culture may be, our favorite novels, movies, and recordings were not all produced just yesterday. Anyone's favorite epochs, including those of the cultural optimist, will lie at some point in the past. As a result, each field will appear to have declined, given that some superior era lies behind us in each case. Yet we should not conclude that creativity is drying up or slowing down. Rather, the past contains more accumulated achievement than does any single moment in time, such as the present. Furthermore, cultural pessimism will appear increasingly persuasive, precisely because the world continues to produce creative works. With every passing year, the entire past contains an increasing amount of culture, relative to the present.

No Reason for Cultural Pessimism

Laments about cultural decline echo through history. Listen to this 1808 European observer on the tragedy of the proliferation of popular novels through circulating libraries: "There is scarcely a street of the metropolis, or a village in the country, in which a circulating library may not be found: nor is there a corner of the empire, where the English language is understood, that has not suffered from the effects of this institution."

Today, we focus on some foul-mouthed rapper as if he were the sum total of all that we do and think, look at and listen to—as if he were somehow more representative of our culture than Duke Ellington or Martha Graham or Alfred Hitchcock.

Only history will sift out the great voices of our era, as it has from other eras. But we do have them, just as previous centuries had their Jerry Springer equivalents.

Geneva Overholser, *Washington Post*, February 16, 1999.

We also consume contemporary culture less efficiently than we consume the culture of the past. Eighteenth-century music critics did not commonly understand that Haydn and Mozart were categorically superior to Gluck, Cherubini, Cimarosa, and Gretry. Years of debate and listening were needed for the truth to become obvious. Similarly, we cannot yet identify the truly worthy and seminal performers in modern popular music or contemporary art. It takes decades, and sometimes even centuries, to separate the cultural wheat from the chaff.

Most great creators, even those who now strike us as conservative, faced considerable opposition in their day. The French Impressionists were rejected by the artistic mainstream of their day and considered ridiculously unstructured. Mozart's music was considered incredibly dissonant by many of his contemporaries. One critic charged Anton Bruckner with being "the greatest living musical peril, a tonal Antichrist . . . [who] composes nothing but high treason, revolution and murder . . . poisoned with the sulphur of Hell."

Older audiences often cannot appreciate new and innovative cultural products. Many individuals devote their maximum attention to culture in their youth. Between the ages of 15 and 25, for instance, the mind is receptive to new influences, individuals are searching for their identity, and, more often than not, they are rebelling against their elders. For many individuals, those years are a formative period for cultural taste. Over time, however, marriage, children, and jobs crowd out the opportunity to discover new products. Therefore, in the eyes of many individuals, culture appears to be drying up and declining, which creates yet further support for pessimism.

Some individuals hold pessimistic attitudes to support their elitism. Elitists need to feel that they belong to a privileged minority. Contemporary culture, however, is massive in size, diverse in scope, and widely disseminated. Elitists have a hard time sustaining their self-images if they admit that our culture is wonderful and vibrant. Celebrating the dynamism of modern creations ascribes aesthetic virtues and insights to a very large class of artistic producers and consumers—contra elitism.

The diversity of modern culture implies that much trash will be produced, providing fodder for pessimism and elitism. We should keep these low-quality outputs in perspective and view them as a luxury that only diverse and wealthy societies can afford.

"Resource Pessimism"

Some kinds of cultural pessimism spring from lack of imagination. Cultural pessimism and "resource pessimism" share common roots in this regard. Resource pessimism is the view, effectively criticized by Julian Simon, that the world will run out of resources in the near future. Resource pessimists focus on one kind of resource, such as oil, and see only so many years' supply remaining. They fail to see that the world could procure energy by different means in the future. Many cultural pessimists hold analogous attitudes. The West has developed certain great art forms, such as epic poetry, classical drama, and the symphony. Those forms have been "exhausted," at least in terms of the taste of the pessimist, implying cultural decline. Yet we should not look for cultural innovation to recur in the same areas over time; if anything, we should expect the exact opposite. There is no 20th-century Homer or Aeschylus, but we do have Alfred Hitchcock, Duke Ellington, and Frank Lloyd Wright.

Cultural pessimism has been around as long as culture. Pessimistic attacks have been leveled for centuries, although the target has changed frequently. Many moralists and philosophers, including Plato, criticized theater and poetry for their corrupting influence. Books became a target after the onset of publishing. Eighteenth-century pessimists accused novels of preventing readers from thinking, preaching disobedience to parents (note the contradictory charges), undermining women's sense of subservience, breaking down class distinctions, and making readers sick. Libraries, especially privately run circulating libraries, were another target. Edward Mangin remarked in 1808, "There is scarcely a street of the metropolis, or a village in the country, in which a circulating library may not be found: nor is there a corner of the empire, where the English language is understood, that has not suffered from the effects of this institution."

In the 18th and 19th centuries the targets included epistolary romances, newspapers, opera, the music hall, photography, and instrumental virtuosi, such as Liszt and Paganini. The 20th century brought the scapegoats of radio, movies, modern art, professional sports, the automobile, television, rhythm and blues, rock 'n' roll, comic books, MTV music videos, and rap music. Each new medium or genre has been accused of corrupting youth and promoting excess sensuality, political subversion, and moral relativism.

My version of cultural optimism offers a contrasting perspective. Capitalist art consists fundamentally of bringing the consumer and producer together. Therein lies its exhilarating, challenging, and poetic nature. Marketplace art is about the meeting of minds and hearts. We should not deplore our culture, as do the pessimists. Rather, we should recognize its fundamentally capitalist nature, which implies creativity, entertainment, innovation, and above all diversity.

"[We Americans] trade our individuality and our passion for the distraction of material things."

Consumerism Pervades American Society

David Klepper

In the subsequent viewpoint, David Klepper, a student at the University of Illinois at Urbana-Champaign at the time this viewpoint was written, asserts that consumerism has become the driving force of American society. According to Klepper, Americans are fixated on the mindless and never-ending pursuit of material satisfaction.

As you read, consider the following questions:
1. Who is to blame for numbing Americans' minds, in Klepper's opinion?
2. According to the author, how has society been tainted by consumerism?

Excerpted from "Big Brother Is on Your Shoes," by David Klepper, *University Wire*, June 22, 1999. Reprinted with permission from the author.

June 1999 was the 50th anniversary of the release of *1984*, by George Orwell. He wrote it as a caution to various social and political trends he saw amassing strength in postwar Europe. He foresaw a large, fascist bureaucracy that controlled the lives of its citizens through mind-numbing social conditioning, paranoia and constant surveillance. This government, Big Brother, not only wanted the taxes and votes of its citizenry, but also their freedom, their minds and their individuality. It's a spooky book, one that cannot be dismissed as mere *X-File*-ish, conspiracy drivel. Fifty years later, *1984* is still relevant, still terrifying in its critique of a homogenizing, demeaning and deluding world order.

1984 is about the troubles of one man who grows tired of Big Brother's constant surveillance and social control. His civilization, which is constantly at war with one of two other world powers, is divided into two socio-economic groups. These groups are the proles, short for members of the proletariat, and the Party Members. All Party Members are watched constantly by the all-seeing telescreens, and are held in check by terrifying paranoia. Any deviance from Big Brother's Party line, such as the very mention of the words "God" or "Freedom," even in private conversation, is punishable by swift interrogation and death.

One character is carried away by the secret police because he once utters a condemnation of Big Brother in his sleep. His children hear him and turn him in. Family bonds, sexual relationships and even private thoughts and wishes are viewed as dissident behavior and are punished rapidly. As a result, people lost their ability to love, to hate, to yearn and to think for themselves.

Overcome by the Mighty Dollar

Most American readers of *1984* rest assured that this fascist regime could never happen here. They believe Americans, as individualistic and freedom-loving as we claim to be, could never allow this to happen. And they're right, sort of. Americans will not be executed or tortured. We are too soft for those kinds of things—instead, we will be overcome by the Mighty Dollar, the Hardee's Star and the ever-advancing column of fads.

STaR of BeTHLeHeM

Kirk Anderson. Reprinted with permission.

Orwell got it wrong when he laid the blame for the night-mare of *1984* on the government. It's not the government that is numbing our minds, turning us into blind consumers and television-dumbed vegetables. It's the commercialism and consumerism that fuels America nowadays. It's the fault of Nike, McDonald's and Hollywood big shots. And it's our fault. We're the ones who tune in to the television and turn off our minds. We have heated conversations about which is better, Coke or Pepsi. We wear shirts with a swoosh, just for the swoosh. I don't believe these corporations intend to steal our individuality; they're just trying to corner the market and make a few bucks. But somewhere along the way, capitalism has turned us from citizens into consumers, who consume because it is what our economy demands. After all, it's good for business—we all make more money to spend on more junk.

The Taint of Consumerism

Everything has been tainted by this consumerism. Commercials are now art and art is now commercialized— advertisements are discussed and debated for their merits while art is judged by how many copies have been sold or how many people tuned in to watch. We pay $45 for a shirt with a special logo and shell out hundreds for little yellow stitches on a pair of shoes.

We always want more—we satisfy ourselves with new clothes, new cars, new trinkets. Songs are picked by record companies and radio stations because they are catchy and memorable—for two weeks. And then, the song self-destructs, becomes boring and old, and is promptly replaced by another equally vacuous and catchy song. This is designed to happen, to ensure the fast turnover of CDs. Same with movies. And same with TV.

Does anyone else worry about this? I'm sure that if someone from a century ago were to visit us now in 1999, he would be shocked by our devolution. Sure, maybe we're smarter, more informed. We can all read. But we don't —instead we trade our individuality and our passion for the distraction of material things. Nietzsche said religion made us weak, sapped our wills. Well, God has been eclipsed by the boob tube and that stupid Taco Bell Chihuahua. Television is mostly to blame. But you, reader, should pat yourself on the back. Good for you for actually reading a newspaper, though the media is also partly responsible for the numbing of America. But at least you're reading, and not watching the damn television. Turn it off. Take off those hip shoes and go outside. Enjoy the summer, and try, maybe just for a week, to limit your purchases to the necessities—food and beer.

"Getting and spending has become the most passionate, and often the most imaginative, endeavor of modern life."

Consumerism Can Be a Positive Force

James B. Twitchell

James B. Twitchell, a professor of English at the University of Florida, Gainesville, writes in the following viewpoint that consumerism is, in many ways, a positive force in American society. According to Twitchell, the number of choices available to American consumers makes them feel emancipated and powerful. Furthermore, he contends, the process of consumption can be both pleasurable and meaningful. Twitchell is the author of several books, including *Adcult USA: The Triumph of Advertising in American Culture* and *Lead Us Into Temptation: The Triumph of American Materialism*.

As you read, consider the following questions:
1. Why has consumerism proved potent, in Twitchell's opinion?
2. What is the relationship between democracy and consumerism, as explained by the author?
3. According to the author, how has consumer culture freed people from the strictures of social class?

Excerpted from "It's a Material World, and That's OK," by James B. Twitchell, *Wilson Quarterly*, Spring 1999. Reprinted with permission from the author.

O f all the strange beasts that have come slouching into the 20th century, none has been more misunderstood, more criticized, and more important than materialism. Who but fools, toadies, hacks, and occasional loopy libertarians have ever risen to its defense? Yet the fact remains that while materialism may be the most shallow of the 20th century's various -isms, it has been the one that has ultimately triumphed. The world of commodities appears so antithetical to the world of ideas that it seems almost heresy to point out the obvious: most of the world most of the time spends most of its energy producing and consuming more and more stuff. The really interesting question may be not why we are so materialistic, but why we are so unwilling to acknowledge and explore what seems the central characteristic of modern life.

When the French wished to disparage the English in the 19th century, they called them a nation of shopkeepers. When the rest of the world now wishes to disparage Americans, they call us a nation of consumers. And they are right. We are developing and rapidly exporting a new material culture, a mallcondo culture. To the rest of the world we do indeed seem not just born to shop, but alive to shop. Americans spend more time tooling around the mallcondo—three to four times as many hours as our European counterparts—and we have more stuff to show for it. According to some estimates, we have about four times as many things as Middle Europeans, and who knows how much more than people in the less developed parts of the world. The quantity and disparity are increasing daily, even though, as we see in Russia and China, the "emerging nations" are playing a frantic game of catch-up.

This burst of mallcondo commercialism has happened recently—in my lifetime—and it is spreading around the world at the speed of television. The average American consumes twice as many goods and services as in 1950; in fact, the poorest fifth of the current population buys more than the average fifth did in 1955. Little wonder that the average new home of today is twice as large as the average house built in the early years after World War II. We have to put that stuff somewhere—quick!—before it turns to junk.

Sooner or later we are going to have to acknowledge the

uncomfortable fact that this amoral consumerama has proved potent because human beings love things. In fact, to a considerable degree we live for things. In all cultures we buy things, steal things, exchange things, and horde things. From time to time, some of us collect vast amounts of things, from tulip bulbs to paint drippings on canvasses to matchbook covers. Often these objects have no observable use.

We live through things. We create ourselves through things. And we change ourselves by changing our things. In the West, we have even developed the elaborate algebra of commercial law to decide how things are exchanged, divested, and recaptured. Remember, we call these things "goods," as in "goods and services." We don't—unless we are academic critics—call them "bads." This sounds simplistic, but it is crucial to understanding the powerful allure of materialism.

Our commercial culture has been blamed for the rise of eating disorders, the spread of "affluenza," the epidemic of depression, the despoliation of cultural icons, the corruption of politics, the carnivalization of holy times like Christmas, and the gnat-life attention span of our youth. All of this is true. Commercialism contributes. But it is by no means the whole truth. Commercialism is more a mirror than a lamp. In demonizing it, in seeing ourselves as helpless and innocent victims of its overpowering force, in making it the scapegoat du jour, we reveal far more about our own eagerness to be passive in the face of complexity than about the thing itself. . . .

The Right to Buy Anything You Want

If you want to understand the potency of American consumer culture, ask any group of teenagers what democracy means to them. You will hear an extraordinary response. Democracy is the right to buy anything you want. Freedom's just another word for lots of things to buy. Appalling perhaps, but there is something to their answer. Being able to buy what you want when and where you want it was, after all, the right that made 1989 a watershed year in Eastern Europe.

Recall as well that freedom to shop was another way to describe the right to be served in a restaurant that provided one focus for the early civil rights movement. Go back further. It was the right to consume freely which sparked the fires of separation of this country from England. The freedom to buy what you want (even if you can't pay for it) is what most foreigners immediately spot as what they like about our culture, even though in the next breath they will understandably criticize it.

The Truth About Materialism

Look at the pathetic offerings of the anti-materialists, the limp "anti" philosophy of lines like, "Money can't buy love" and "Money can't buy happiness." Lies we tell on the way to the mall.

We ought to just own up to the truth: Wealth may not buy love, but it's a much better come-on than poverty. We can admit that wealth buys admiration, attention, mates.

And while money can't buy happiness, it can buy pleasures, and as long as you're stringing together new and better pleasures, you're happy.

Dale Dauten, *St. Louis Post-Dispatch*, November 24, 1997.

The pressure to commercialize—to turn things into commodities and then market them as charms—has always been particularly Western. As Max Weber first argued in *The Protestant Ethic and the Spirit of Capitalism* (1905), much of the Protestant Reformation was geared toward denying the holiness of many things that the Catholic church had endowed with meanings. From the inviolable priesthood to the sacrificial holy water, this deconstructive movement systematically unloaded meaning. Soon the marketplace would capture this off-loaded meaning and apply it to secular things. Buy this, you'll be saved. You deserve a break today. You, you're the one. We are the company that cares about you. You're worth it. You are in good hands. We care. Trust in us. We are here for you.

Materialism, it's important to note, does not crowd out spiritualism; spiritualism is more likely a substitute when objects are scarce. When we have few things we make the next world holy. When we have plenty we enchant the objects around us. The hereafter becomes the here and now.

We have not grown weaker but stronger by accepting the

self-evidently ridiculous myths that sacramentalize mass-produced objects; we have not wasted away but have proved inordinately powerful; have not devolved and been rebarbarized, but seem to have marginally improved. Dreaded affluenza notwithstanding, commercialism has lessened pain. Most of us have more pleasure and less discomfort in our lives than most of the people most of the time in all of history. . . .

The process of consumption is creative and even emancipating. In an open market, we consume the real and the imaginary meanings, fusing objects, symbols, and images together to end up with "a little world made cunningly." Rather than lives, individuals since midcentury have had lifestyles. For better or worse, lifestyles are secular religions, coherent patterns of valued things. Your lifestyle is not related to what you do for a living but to what you buy. One of the chief aims of the way we live now is the enjoyment of affiliating with those who share the same clusters of objects as we do.

Mallcondo culture is so powerful in part because it frees us from the strictures of social class. The outcome of material life is no longer preordained by coat of arms, pew seat, or trust fund. Instead, it evolves from a never-ending shifting of individual choice. No one wants to be middle class, for instance. You want to be cool, hip, with it, with the "in" crowd, instead.

One of the reasons terms like Yuppie, Baby Boomer, and GenX have elbowed aside such older designations as "upper middle class" is that we no longer understand social class as well as we do lifestyle, or what marketing firms call "consumption communities." Observing stuff is the way we understand each other. Even if no one knows exactly how much money it takes to be a yuppie, or how young you have to be, or how upwardly aspiring, everybody knows where yuppies gather, how they dress, what they play, what they drive, what they eat, and why they hate to be called yuppies.

American Culture as the World Culture

For better or worse, American culture is well on its way to becoming world culture. The Soviets have fallen. Only quixotic French intellectuals and anxious Islamic fundamentalists are trying to stand up to it. By no means am I sanguine about such a material culture. It has many problems that I have glossed over. Consumerism is wasteful, it is devoid of otherworldly concerns, it lives for today and celebrates the body, and it overindulges and spoils the young with impossible promises.

"Getting and spending" has eclipsed family, ethnicity, even religion as a defining matrix. That doesn't mean that those other defining systems have disappeared, but that an increasing number of young people around the world will give more of their loyalty to Nike than to creeds of blood, race, or belief. This is not entirely a bad thing, since a lust for upscale branding isn't likely to drive many people to war, but it is, to say the least, far from inspiring.

It would be nice to think that materialism could be heroic, self-abnegating, and redemptive. It would be nice to think that greater material comforts will release us from racism, sexism, and ethnocentrism, and that the apocalypse will come as it did at the end of romanticism in Shelley's "Prometheus Unbound," leaving us "Scepterless, free, uncircumscribed . . . Equal, unclassed, tribeless, and nationless."

But it is more likely that the globalization of capitalism will result in the banalities of an ever-increasing worldwide consumerist culture. The French don't stand a chance. The untranscendent, repetitive, sensational, democratic, immediate, tribalizing and unifying force of what Irving Kristol calls the American Imperium need not necessarily result in a Bronze Age of culture. But it certainly will not produce what Shelley had in mind.

We have not been led into this world of material closeness against our better judgment. For many of us, especially when young, consumerism is our better judgment. We have not just asked to go this way, we have demanded. Now most of the world is lining up, pushing and shoving, eager to elbow into the mall. Getting and spending has become the most passionate, and often the most imaginative, endeavor of modern life. While this is dreary and depressing to some, as doubtless it should be, it is liberating and democratic to many more.

Periodical Bibliography

The following articles have been selected to supplement the diverse views presented in this chapter. Addresses are provided for periodicals not indexed in the *Readers' Guide to Periodical Literature*, the *Alternative Press Index*, the *Social Sciences Index*, or the *Index to Legal Periodicals and Books*.

William J. Bennett — "Why It Matters," *Wall Street Journal*, March 6, 1998.

Paul Ekins — "From Consumption to Satisfaction," *Resurgence*, November/December 1998. Available from Small Changes, 316 Terry Ave. N., PO Box 19046, Seattle, WA 98109.

Mark Gauvreau Judge — "America's Sexual Right Turn," *Insight*, June 2, 1997. Available from 3600 New York Ave. NE, Washington, DC 20002.

John B. Judis — "Value-Free: How Capitalism Redefines Morality," *New Republic*, April 26–May 3, 1999.

Everett Carll Ladd — "The American Way—Civic Engagement—Thrives," *Christian Science Monitor*, March 1, 1999.

Stanley Lebergott — "Consuming Passion," *New York Times*, February 10, 1998.

John Leo — "The Joy of Sexual Values," *U.S. News & World Report*, March 1, 1999.

Robert D. Putnam and Nancy Day — "Our Separate Ways," *People Weekly*, September 25, 1995.

Christina Hoff Sommers — "Why Johnny Can't Tell Right from Wrong," *American Outlook*, Summer 1998. Available from the Hudson Institute, PO Box 26–919, Indianapolis, IN 46226.

Stephen Joel Trachtenberg — "The Collapse That Didn't," *World & I*, June 1998. Available from 3400 New York Ave. NE, Washington, DC 20002.

David Wagner — "No Morality, No Problem?" *Insight*, April 27, 1998.

Robert Weissberg — "The Abduction of Tolerance," *Society*, November/December 1998.

David Whitman, Paul Glastris, and Brendan I. Koerner — "Was It Good for Us?" *U.S. News & World Report*, May 19, 1997.

Alan Wolfe — "Is Civil Society Obsolete?" *Brookings Review*, Fall 1997.

Karl Zinsmeister, Stephen Moore, and Karlyn Bowman — "Is America Turning a Corner?" *American Enterprise*, January/February 1999. Available from 1150 17th St. NW, Washington, DC 20036.

CHAPTER 3

How Do the Media Influence American Values?

Chapter Preface

On April 20, 1999, in what turned out to be the worst school shooting in the nation's history, students Eric Harris and Dylan Klebold opened fire on their classmates at Columbine High in Littleton, Colorado, killing twelve students and one teacher before committing suicide. Survivors of the massacre reported that the killers—apparently motivated by revenge—had laughed gleefully as they stalked and murdered their victims.

In the view of some commentators, the Columbine killings share a disturbing similarity with the 1995 movie *The Basketball Diaries*, in which the main character, played by Leonardo DiCaprio, is cheered on by friends as he guns down students who had taunted him. Columnist Terry Teachout states that "to watch that horrific clip is to know in your bones that Harris and Klebold must also have seen it at some point in their short, sad lives, and felt the dark urge to go and do likewise." Others who believe media violence may have inspired Harris and Klebold's actions note that the teenagers were fans of the point-and-shoot video game "Doom," and had even configured the game's settings to resemble the floor plan of Columbine High.

However, others maintain that criticisms of media violence are misplaced. As writer Adam Gopnick explains, "Well-meaning people turn to culture to explain violence because they want a deeper explanation than '[Harris and Klebold] were sick, and they bought bombs and guns.' . . . The right reaction to Littleton may be the most superficial one: grief and gun control." Those who disagree that media violence has a negative impact point out that only an infinitesimal proportion of those who view images of violence actually commit violent crimes; in addition, they claim, people who perpetrate atrocities such as the one in Littleton are disturbed human beings who would have acted violently without the influence of media.

The authors in the following chapter debate the effects of movie and television violence on society, and offer conflicting views on how entertainment media influence America's values.

"In cinema's never-ending quest to up the ante on violence, murder as sport is the latest frontier."

The Media Glamorize Violence

Gregg Easterbrook

In the following viewpoint, Gregg Easterbrook, a senior editor at the *New Republic* magazine, argues that the movie industry glamorizes violence by portraying murder as a thrilling, daredevil "sport" and by associating firearms with sexual potency. For viewers who are impressionable or mentally imbalanced, Easterbrook contends, these glamorized images of violence may encourage aggressive behavior.

As you read, consider the following questions:
1. In what ways does the movie industry portray murder as sport, according to Easterbrook?
2. As cited by the author, what does research show about the relationship between media violence and actual violence?
3. What solution does Easterbrook offer to the problem of media violence?

Millions of teens have seen the 1996 movie *Scream*, a box-office and home-rental hit. Critics adored the film. The *Washington Post* declared that it "deftly mixes irony, self-reference, and social wry commentary." The *Los Angeles Times* hailed it as "a bravura, provocative send-up." *Scream* opens with a scene in which a teenage girl is forced to watch her jock boyfriend tortured and then disemboweled by two fellow students who, it will eventually be learned, want revenge on anyone from high school who crossed them. After jock boy's stomach is shown cut open and he dies screaming, the killers stab and torture the girl, then cut her throat and hang her body from a tree so that Mom can discover it when she drives up. A dozen students and teachers are graphically butchered in the film, while the characters make running jokes about murder. At one point, a boy tells a big-breasted friend she'd better be careful because the stacked girls always get it in horror films; in the next scene, she's grabbed, stabbed through the breasts, and murdered. Some provocative send-up, huh? The movie builds to a finale in which one of the killers announces that he and his accomplice started off by murdering strangers but then realized it was a lot more fun to kill their friends.

Now that two Colorado high schoolers have murdered twelve classmates and a teacher—often, it appears, first taunting their pleading victims, just like celebrity stars do in the movies!—some commentators have dismissed the role of violence in the images shown to the young, pointing out that horrific acts by children existed before celluloid or the phosphor screen. That is true—the Leopold-Loeb murder of 1924, for example. But mass murders by the young, once phenomenally rare, are suddenly on the increase. Can it be coincidence that this increase is happening at the same time that Hollywood has begun to market the notion that mass murder is fun?

For, in cinema's never-ending quest to up the ante on violence, murder as sport is the latest frontier. Slasher flicks began this trend; most portray carnage from the killer's point of view, showing the victim cowering, begging, screaming as the blade goes in, treating each death as a moment of festivity for the killer. (Many killers seek feelings of power over their victims, criminology finds; by reveling in the pleas of victims, slasher movies promote this base emotion.) The 1994 movie *Natural Born Killers* depicted slaying the helpless not only as a way to have a grand time but also as a way to become a celebrity; several dozen on-screen murders are shown in that film, along with a discussion of how great it makes you feel to just pick people out at random and kill them. The 1994 movie *Pulp Fiction* presented hit men as glamour figures having loads of interesting fun; the actors were mainstream stars like John Travolta. The 1995 movie *Seven*, starring Brad Pitt, portrayed a sort of contest to murder in unusually grotesque ways. (Screenwriters now actually discuss, and critics comment on, which film's killings are most amusing.) The 1995 movie *The Basketball Diaries* contains an extended dream sequence in which the title character, played by teen heartthrob Leonardo DiCaprio, methodically guns down whimpering, pleading classmates at his high school. A rock soundtrack pulses, and the character smiles as he kills.

Profiting from Gratuitous Violence

The new Hollywood tack of portraying random murder as a form of recreation does not come from schlock-houses. Disney's Miramax division, the same mainstream studio that produced *Shakespeare in Love*, is responsible for *Scream* and *Pulp Fiction*. Time-Warner is to blame for *Natural Born Killers* and actually ran television ads promoting this film as "delirious, daredevil fun." (After it was criticized for calling murder "fun," Time-Warner tried to justify *Killers* as social commentary; if you believe that, you believe *Godzilla* was really about biodiversity protection.) Praise and publicity for gratuitously violent movies come from the big media conglomerates, including the newspapers and networks that profit from advertising for films that glorify murder. Disney, now one of the leading promoters of violent images in American culture, even feels that what little kids need is more violence. Its Christmas 1998 children's movie *Mighty Joe Young* begins with an eight-year-old girl watching her mother being murdered. By the movie's end, it is 20 years later, and the killer has returned to stalk the grown daughter, pointing a gun in her face and announcing, "Now join your mother in hell." A Disney movie.

One reason Hollywood keeps reaching for ever-more-obscene levels of killing is that it must compete with television, which today routinely airs the kind of violence once considered shocking in theaters. According to studies conducted at Temple University, prime-time network (non-news) shows now average up to five violent acts per hour. In February 1999, NBC ran in prime time the movie *Eraser*, not editing out an extremely graphic scene in which a killer pulls a gun on a bystander and blasts away. The latest TV movie based on *The Rockford Files*, which aired on CBS the night of the Colorado murders, opened with a scene of an eleven-year-old girl in short-shorts being stalked by a man in a black hood, grabbed, and dragged off, screaming. *The Rockford Files* is a comedy. Combining television and movies, the typical American boy or girl, studies find, will observe a stunning 40,000 dramatizations of killing by age 18.

In the days after the Colorado slaughter, discussion of violent images in American culture was dominated by the canned positions of the anti-Hollywood right and the mammon-is-our-God film lobby. The debate missed three vital points: the distinction between what adults should be allowed to see (anything) and what the inchoate minds of children and adolescents should see; the way in which important liberal battles to win free expression in art and literature have been perverted into an excuse for antisocial video brutality produced by cynical capitalists; and the difference between censorship and voluntary acts of responsibility.

The day after the Colorado shooting, Mike De Luca, an executive of New Line Cinema, maker of *The Basketball Diaries*, told *USA Today* that, when kids kill, "bad home life, bad parenting, having guns in the home" are "more of a factor than what we put out there for entertainment." Setting aside the disclosure that Hollywood now categorizes scenes of movie stars gunning down the innocent as "entertainment," De Luca is correct: studies do show that upbringing is more determinant of violent behavior than any other factor. But research also clearly shows that the viewing of violence can cause aggression and crime. So the question is, in a society already plagued by poor parenting and unlimited gun sales, why does the entertainment industry feel privileged to make violence even more prevalent?

Media and the Rise of Violent Crime

Even when researchers factor out other influences such as parental attention, many peer-reviewed studies have found causal links between viewing phony violence and engaging in actual violence. A 1971 surgeon general's report asserted a broad relationship between the two. Studies by Brandon Centerwall, an epidemiologist at the University of Wisconsin, have shown that the postwar murder rise in the United States began roughly a decade after TV viewing became common. Centerwall also found that, in South Africa, where television was not generally available until 1975, national murder rates started rising about a decade later. Violent computer games have not existed long enough to be the subject of many controlled studies, but experts expect it will be shown that playing such games in youth also correlates with destructive behavior. There's an eerie likelihood that violent movies and violent games amplify one another, the film and television images placing thoughts of carnage into the psyche while the games condition the trigger finger to act on those impulses.

Leonard Eron, a psychologist at the University of Michigan, has been tracking video violence and actual violence for almost four decades. His initial studies, in 1960, found that even the occasional violence depicted in 1950s television—to which every parent would gladly return today—caused increased aggression among eight-year-olds. By the adult years, Eron's studies find, those who watched the most TV and movies in childhood were much more likely to have been arrested for, or convicted of, violent felonies. Eron believes that ten percent of U.S. violent crime is caused by exposure to images of violence, meaning that 90 percent is not but that a ten percent national reduction in violence might be achieved merely by moderating the content of television and movies. "Kids learn by observation," Eron says. "If what they observe is violent, that's what they learn." To cite a minor but telling example, the introduction of vulgar language into American public discourse traces, Eron thinks, largely to the point at which stars like Clark Gable began to swear onscreen, and kids then imitated swearing as normative.

Defenders of bloodshed in film, television, and writing often argue that depictions of killing don't incite real violence because no one is really affected by what they see or read; it's all just water off a duck's back. At heart, this is an argument against free expression. The whole reason to have a First Amendment is that people are influenced by what they see and hear: words and images do change minds, so there must be free competition among them. If what we say, write, or show has no consequences, why bother to have free speech?

Defenders of Hollywood bloodshed also employ the argument that, since millions of people watch screen mayhem and shrug, feigned violence has no causal relation to actual violence. After a horrific 1992 case in which a British gang acted out a scene from the slasher movie *Child's Play 3*, torturing a girl to death as the movie had shown, the novelist Martin Amis wrote dismissively in the *New Yorker* that he had rented

Child's Play 3 and watched the film, and it hadn't made him want to kill anyone, so what was the problem? But Amis isn't homicidal or unbalanced. For those on the psychological borderline, the calculus is different. There have, for example, been at least two instances of real-world shootings in which the guilty imitated scenes in *Natural Born Killers*.

Most telling, Amis wasn't affected by watching a slasher movie because Amis is not young. Except for the unbalanced, exposure to violence in video "is not so important for adults; adults can watch anything they want," Eron says. Younger minds are a different story. Children who don't yet understand the difference between illusion and reality may be highly affected by video violence. Between the ages of two and eight, hours of viewing violent TV programs and movies correlates closely to felonies later in life; the child comes to see hitting, stabbing, and shooting as normative acts. The link between watching violence and engaging in violence continues up to about the age of 19, Eron finds, after which most people's characters have been formed, and video mayhem no longer correlates to destructive behavior.

Making Killing Seem Cool

Trends in gun availability do not appear to explain the murder rise that has coincided with television and violent films. Research by John Lott Jr., of the University of Chicago Law School, shows that the percentage of homes with guns has changed little throughout the postwar era. What appears to have changed is the willingness of people to fire their guns at one another. Are adolescents now willing to use guns because violent images make killing seem acceptable or even cool? Following the Colorado slaughter, the *New York Times* ran a recounting of other postwar mass murders staged by the young, such as the 1966 Texas tower killings, and noted that they all happened before the advent of the Internet or shock rock, which seemed to the *Times* to absolve the modern media. But all the mass killings by the young occurred after 1950—after it became common to watch violence on television.

When horrific murders occur, the film and television industries routinely attempt to transfer criticism to the weapons used. Just after the Colorado shootings, for instance, TV talk-show host Rosie O'Donnell called for a constitutional amendment banning all firearms. How strange that O'Donnell didn't call instead for a boycott of Sony or its production company, Columbia Tristar—a film studio from which she has received generous paychecks and whose current offerings include *8MM*, which glamorizes the sexual murder of young women, and *The Replacement Killers*, whose hero is a hit man and which depicts dozens of gun murders. Handguns should be licensed, but that hardly excuses the convenient sanctimony of blaming the crime on the weapon, rather than on what resides in the human mind.

And, when it comes to promoting adoration of guns, Hollywood might as well be the National Rifle Association's (NRA) marketing arm. An ever-increasing share of film and television depicts the firearm as something the virile must have and use, if not an outright sexual aid. Check the theater section of any newspaper, and you will find an ever-higher percentage of movie ads in which the stars are prominently holding guns. Keanu Reeves, Uma Thurman, Laurence Fishburne, Geena Davis, Woody Harrelson, and Mark Wahlberg are just a few of the hip stars who have posed with guns for movie advertising. Hollywood endlessly congratulates itself for reducing the depiction of cigarettes in movies and movie ads. Cigarettes had to go, the film industry admitted, because glamorizing them gives the wrong idea to kids. But the glamorization of firearms, which is far more dangerous, continues. Today, even female stars who otherwise consider themselves politically aware will model in sexualized poses with guns. Ads for the movie *Goodbye Lover* show star Patricia Arquette nearly nude, with very little between her and the viewer but her handgun.

But doesn't video violence merely depict a stark reality against which the young need be warned? American society is far too violent, yet the forms of brutality highlighted in the movies and on television—prominently "thrill" killings and serial murders—are pure distortion. Nearly 99 percent of real murders result from robberies, drug deals, and domestic disputes; figures from research affiliated with the FBI's behavioral sciences division show an average of only about 30 serial or "thrill" murders nationally per year. Thirty is plenty horrifying enough, but, at this point, each of the major networks and movie studios alone depicts more "thrill" and serial murders annually than that. By endlessly exploiting the notion of the "thrill" murder, Hollywood and television present to the young an entirely imaginary image of a society in which killing for pleasure is a common event. The publishing industry, including some [*New Republic*] advertisers, also distorts for profit the frequency of "thrill" murders.

The "Down-Rating" of Movies

The profitability of violent cinema is broadly dependent on the "down-rating" of films—movies containing extreme violence being rated only R instead of NC-17 (the new name for X)—and the lax enforcement of age restrictions regarding movies. Teens are the best market segment for Hollywood; when moviemakers claim their violent movies are not meant to appeal to teens, they are simply lying. The millionaire status of actors, directors, and studio heads—and the returns of the mutual funds that invest in movie companies—depends on not restricting teen access to theaters or film rentals. Studios in effect control the movie ratings board and endlessly lobby it not to label extreme violence with an NC-17, the only form of rating that is actually enforced. *Natural Born Killers*, for example, received an R following Time-Warner lobbying, despite its repeated close-up murders and one charming scene in which the stars kidnap a high school girl and argue about whether it would be more fun to kill her before or after raping her. Since its inception, the movie ratings board has put its most restrictive rating on any realistic representation of lovemaking, while sanctioning ever-more-graphic depictions of murder and torture. In economic terms, the board's pro-violence bias gives studios an incentive to present more death and mayhem, confident that ratings officials will smile with approval.

When R-and-X battles were first fought, intellectual sentiment regarded the ratings system as a way of blocking the young from seeing films with political content, such as *Easy Rider*, or discouraging depictions of sexuality; ratings were perceived as the rubes' counterattack against cinematic sophistication. But, in the 1960s, murder after murder after murder was not standard cinema fare. The most controversial violent film of that era, *A Clockwork Orange*, depicted a total of one killing, which was heard but not on-camera. (*Clockwork Orange* also had genuine political content, unlike most of today's big-studio movies.) In an era of runaway screen violence, the '60s ideal that the young should be allowed to see what they want has been corrupted. In this, trends in video mirror the misuse of liberal ideals generally.

Anti-censorship battles of this century were fought on firm ground, advocating the right of films to tackle social and sexual issues (the 1930s Hays office forbid among other things cinematic mention of cohabitation) and free access to works of literature such as *Ulysses*, *Story of O*, and the original version of Norman Mailer's *The Naked and the Dead*. Struggles against censors established that suppression of film or writing is wrong.

But to say that nothing should be censored is very different from saying that everything should be shown. Today, Hollywood and television have twisted the First Amendment concept that occasional repulsive or worthless expression must be protected, so as to guarantee freedom for works of genuine political content or artistic merit, into a new standard in which constitutional freedoms are employed mainly to safeguard works that make no pretense of merit. In the new standard, the bulk of what's being protected is repulsive or worthless, with the meritorious work the rare exception.

Not only is there profit for the performers, producers, management, and shareholders of firms that glorify violence, so, too, is there profit for politicians. Many conservative or Republican politicians who denounce Hollywood eagerly accept its lucre. Bob Dole's 1995 anti-Hollywood speech was not followed up by any anti-Hollywood legislation or campaign-funds strategy. After the Colorado murders, President Clinton declared, "Parents should take this moment to ask what else they can do to shield children from violent images and experiences that warp young perceptions." But Clinton was careful to avoid criticizing Hollywood, one of the top sources of public backing and campaign contributions for him and his would-be successor, Vice President Al Gore. The president had nothing specific

143

to propose on film violence—only that parents should try to figure out what to do.

Placing Social Responsibility Before Profit

When television producers say it is the parents' obligation to keep children away from the tube, they reach the self-satire point of warning that their own product is unsuitable for consumption. The situation will improve somewhat beginning in 2000, by which time all new TVs must be sold with the "V chip"—supported by Clinton and Gore—which will allow parents to block violent shows. But it will be at least a decade before the majority of the nation's sets include the chip, and who knows how adept young minds will prove at defeating it? Rather than relying on a technical fix that will take many years to achieve an effect, TV producers could simply stop churning out the gratuitous violence. Television could dramatically reduce its output of scenes of killing and still depict violence in news broadcasts, documentaries, and the occasional show in which the horrible is genuinely relevant. Reduction in violence is not censorship; it is placing social responsibility before profit.

The movie industry could practice the same kind of restraint without sacrificing profitability. In this regard, the big Hollywood studios, including Disney, look craven and exploitative compared to, of all things, the porn-video industry. Repulsive material occurs in underground porn, but, in the products sold by the mainstream triple-X distributors such as Vivid Video (the MGM of the erotica business), violence is never, ever, ever depicted—because that would be irresponsible. Women and men perform every conceivable explicit act in today's mainstream porn, but what is shown is always consensual and almost sunnily friendly. Scenes of rape or sexual menace never occur, and scenes of sexual murder are an absolute taboo.

It is beyond irony that today Sony and Time-Warner eagerly market explicit depictions of women being raped, sexually assaulted, and sexually murdered, while the mainstream porn industry would never dream of doing so. But, if money is all that matters, the point here is that mainstream porn is violence-free and yet risqué and highly profitable.

Surely this shows that Hollywood could voluntarily step back from the abyss of glorifying violence and still retain its edge and its income.

Following the Colorado massacre, Republican presidential candidate Gary Bauer declared to a campaign audience, "In the America I want, all of these producers and directors, they would not be able to show their faces in public" because fingers "would be pointing at them and saying, 'Shame, shame.'" The statement sent chills through anyone fearing right-wing thought-control. But Bauer's final clause is correct—Hollywood and television do need to hear the words "shame, shame." The cause of the shame should be removed voluntarily, not to stave off censorship, but because it is the responsible thing to do.

Put it this way. The day after a teenager guns down the sons and daughters of studio executives in a high school in Bel Air or Westwood, Disney and Time-Warner will stop glamorizing murder. Do we have to wait until that day?

| "*The tragic deterioration of U.S. families in recent years has almost nothing to do with entertainment.*"

The Media Are Unfairly Criticized

Danny Goldberg

Danny Goldberg maintains in the following viewpoint that the amount of violent or sexual behavior portrayed by the media is vastly overstated by elite critics who view all forms of popular entertainment as "poison." In reality, contends Goldberg, media entertainment varies widely in quality and should be evaluated on an individual basis. Goldberg is the Chairman and CEO of the Mercury Record Group and the copublisher of *Tikkun* magazine.

As you read, consider the following questions:
1. According to Goldberg, what is the "message theory" of entertainment, and why is this theory false?
2. What evidence does the author provide for why entertainment is not responsible for the deterioration of U.S. families?
3. Why is the comparison between violent entertainment and tobacco invalid, in the author's view?

Excerpted from "Is Pop Culture Poisonous?" by Danny Goldberg, *Tikkun*, September/October 1998. Reprinted with the permission of *Tikkun: A Bimonthly Jewish Critique of Politics, Culture, & Society.*

Cornel West is a great friend of *Tikkun*, an inspired American progressive, and one of my heroes. His new book, written with Sylvia Ann Hewlett, *The War Against Parents*, was excerpted in 1998 by *Tikkun*, and contains some very important arguments about the need to change U.S. laws and culture to support parents and parenting.

However, the chapter in the book titled "A Poisonous Popular Culture" echoes a long parade of attacks on modern entertainment from thinkers and political figures on the Left including Amitai Etzioni, Maya Angelou, and Maryann Medzian, as well as Democratic politicians Senator Joseph Lieberman, ex-Senator Paul Simon, and Congressman Ed Markey. With the exception of a few caveats attacking racism, homophobia, and patriarchy, leftist attacks on entertainment are in perfect sync with similar attacks from cultural conservatives such as Allen Bloom, William Bennett, Robert Bork, and former Vice President Dan Quayle.

Although Quayle coined the phrase "cultural elite" to condemn a supposed cabal of entertainment executives that would make TV character Murphy Brown a single mother, the truly unified elite is a bi-partisan sociological elite consisting of politicos, academics, religious leaders, and journalists who unanimously condemn popular entertainment culture despite the obvious enthusiasm tens of millions of Americans have for various forms of show business. College-educated, upper-middle class or above, and mostly middle-aged, this elite is convinced that their collective taste is not merely aesthetically more enlightened than that of the masses, but morally superior as well.

I do not propose to defend every compact disc, movie, or television show. Like any other community of thousands, there are plenty of evil, stupid, and amoral people in the entertainment business, and among a hundred million or so regular U.S. consumers of popular culture there is plenty of bad behavior. There is nothing wrong with moral criticism of entertainment—indeed, that is precisely what the best critics bring to their work. The fans, executives, and artists alike who care most passionately about art and entertainment invariably include moral criteria in their discussions and arguments about show business.

As a parent of two myself, I don't doubt that interviews with parents turn up criticism of entertainment. Plenty of kid-focused entertainment irritates me (especially those toy commercials!). I'm all for serious discussions of how to regulate what children are exposed to at various ages, and I'd be happy to pay more taxes for more educational TV programs like "Bill Nye the Science Guy."

Sweeping Generalizations About Pop Culture

The problem with elitist attacks on entertainment like Hewlett and West's "A Poisonous Popular Culture" is that they are based on sweeping generalizations that disregard both the artistic context of entertainment's creation and the cultural context of its consumption.

The epitome of this know-nothing approach to entertainment-bashing was Senator Bob Dole's attack on popular music and movies as part of his 1996 presidential campaign. In response to questions after a speech in which the senator attacked by name several films and albums, an aide to Dole immediately and sheepishly admitted that the senator had never seen or heard any of the stigmatized works himself but had relied on researchers. Dole's attack was quickly triangulated by Clinton and Gore, who, also having neither seen nor heard any of the supposedly offensive works, nonetheless agreed with him. (Disclosure: I was Chairman of Warner Bros. Records at the time of Dole's speech, which also attacked parent company Time-Warner.)

Besides calling popular culture "poisonous," the otherwise genteel Hewlett and West, and the people they choose to quote, refer to "rudeness and crudeness," and "a parent-hurting entertainment media." They state flatly, "The entertainment media has moved from celebrating to denigrating parental role and function," and that "Hollywood feeds off psychobabble, narcissistic individualism, and market-driven hedonism." Politicians are attacked for failing to act more vigorously in regulating "television . . . or the internet for that matter . . . yielding to pressure from the entertainment industry."

Apparently, it is not enough to attack certain entertainment products; the people who produce them must also be demonized. Isn't it possible that some artists and entertainment executives share the morals of Hewlett and West but simply have different opinions about entertainment? For example, Hewlett and West devote several hundred words to an attack on the film, *The Santa Clause*, because the movie passingly mentions a 900 sex-phone number and one parent blamed the film for the fact that his daughter spent several hundred dollars calling it. Hewlett and West describe the father of the ten-year-old as being "in agony over his daughter's victimization" and "outraged and bitter" at Disney for making the movie. My wife and I have watched the film with our kids several times. To me, it is one of the most positive Christmas films of the last several years. We never even noticed the reference to the sex-phone number and have never met a parent who did.

The "Message" Theory of Entertainment

At the core of sociological attacks on entertainment is the fallacy that art is meant to be taken literally in a manner similar to religious or political doctrine. Entertainment is described as being a conduit for a "message." Thus, Hewlett and West write: "The media message around parenting is at its most dismissive in contemporary movies where parents are portrayed . . . as bumbling fools." Also from Hewlett and West: "The overwhelming message from progressive liberal folks in Hollywood is—who needs a husband to have a child?" Comparing the supposedly pro-parent Fifties television to today's, Hewlett and West write: "Forty years later, messages . . . are radically different." Describing Oliver Stone's film, *Natural Born Killers*, they write: "The message of this movie does not seem to be cluttered up with uncomfortable consequences." Later on: "Given the messages coming out of the media, it is increasingly difficult for men to derive much self-esteem . . . from the role of husband and father."

With rare exceptions, the "message" theory of entertainment is totally false. Greek and Shakespearean tragedies are not "messages" that life is depressing. Martin Scorsese has directed films with lots of killing and depressed, morally ambiguous protagonists that are nonetheless regularly listed as among the greatest works of cinematic art. Are the film critics less moral than the sociological elite, or are they tuned in to a poetic truth about the dark side of life that great art can sometimes illuminate to the betterment of its audience? B.B. King, the most acclaimed blues guitarist and singer of the last half-century, is notable, among other things, for conveying tremendous joy despite the "down" linear content of the blues lyrics he sings. Moral people all condemn murder, but moral people of good will may disagree about the morality of a particular murder mystery. I always found the horror classics *Dracula* and *Frankenstein* to be kind of creepy, but I do not consider people who love them my moral inferiors.

I am not suggesting that art and entertainment have no impact on culture. The best critics wrestle with the moral subtext of art, as do most passionate fans and the best artists and executives. Hewlett and West's idea of analyzing how the image of parents is expressed in the media is intriguing, but they go about it in a simplistic and absolutist way that states, in essence, that any unflattering depiction of a parent inherently attacks parenthood—and that anyone who disagrees is morally obtuse.

Hewlett and West single out for attack the kid-film comedies *Honey, I Shrunk the Kids* and *Home Alone*, both of which our family also has found to be harmless and enjoyable entertainment. Does this mean we love our children less—or does it simply mean that we happen to have different taste in movies? Comedies are not supposed to be taken literally. Except for political satire, the "message" of a comedy is laughter. It's one thing not to think that a joke is funny. It's another to demonize the jokester and to marginalize people who laugh at the joke.

The Case of *Natural Born Killers*

In extending their critique of what teenagers are attracted to, Hewlett and West walk the well-trod ground of entertainment bashers through the ages. Oliver Stone's *Natural Born Killers*, a favorite target of elitists, is admittedly an edgy movie, and many close friends of mine found it offensive or unwatchable. I respect the sensibility of the film's critics, but, as I see it, to the extent it "comments" on anything, it is an indictment of the news media's exploitation of tragedy, em-

150

bodied in Robert Downey Jr.'s portrayal of a pompous news-caster. It is hard to see how many truly objective critics of *Natural Born Killers* could ignore the fact that it is a black comedy. An impressionistic montage of different film techniques, the film actually includes a sit-com style laugh track for several scenes featuring comedian Rodney Dangerfield. It couldn't be more clear that the film is not meant to be taken literally, but as a poetic cartoon impression of violence, the media, and the U.S.A. circa the 1990s.

A healthy disagreement about a film like *Natural Born Killers* is appropriate, if somewhat out of date. However Hewlett and West direct their energy not to an analysis of the film, but toward the fact that, tragically, several young murderers have been fans of the film. It is a dangerous and unfair argument to blame the movie for the acts of a tiny percentage of its most unstable fans. Charles Manson "credited" the Beatles. More than one serial killer has quoted the Bible. Many depraved murderers, including John Lennon's assassin, Mark David Chapman, have been obsessed with J.D. Salinger's novel *Catcher in the Rye*.

Art is not subordinate to politics or sociology. Abbie Hoffman, A.J. Weberman, and other yippies were wrong when they picketed Bob Dylan's house on the occasion of Dylan's thirtieth birthday, complaining that Dylan had "sold out" by writing more personal songs instead of overtly political ones. There's nothing wrong with encouraging artists to have a social conscience, but pressure from left, right, or center to adhere to a party line is at best pedestrian and at worst philistine.

Misplaced Nostalgia for the Fifties

With generational myopia, Hewlett and West write as if the most popular television shows of the Fifties were about happy families. They acknowledge that the Fifties TV culture mirrored the bigotry of the time, but lament that the culture revolutions that addressed racism and patriarchy "threw out the baby with the bathwater at the expense of pro-family images." *Leave it to Beaver* notwithstanding, however, the dominant genre of Fifties TV was the western. In series such as *Gunsmoke, The Lone Ranger, Hoppalong Cassidy,*

The Rifleman, Have Gun Will Travel, Gene Autry, and *Roy Rogers,* problems were usually solved with violence. Today's rappers refer to their "posse" in direct homage to western dramas. *Ozzie and Harriet* was less a "message" of parental respect than a trojan horse for Ricky Nelson, the TV culture's watered down homage to Elvis Presley. Lucille Ball was famous for her slapstick comedy, not for parenting. As for consumerism, the Fifties were the decade of Davy Crockett coonskin caps and the explosion of quiz shows like *The Price is Right* and *Queen for a Day.*

Yes, TV was different in the Fifties; there were only three networks, each of which had far more power to affect popular culture than does any entity in today's multi-channel cable-TV universe. Although there were certain cultural benefits to a hierarchal popular culture (Leonard Bernstein's classical *Concerts for Young People* comes to mind), there also was an artificial homogeneity of culture that was partially responsible for the Fifties alienation that produced *Mad Magazine,* rock and roll, counter-culture movie stars such as James Dean, Marlon Brando, and Marilyn Monroe, and the literary explosion of the beatniks.

Literalist critics of sex and violence in kids' entertainment mysteriously forget the darkness and complexity of children's art in ages past. One need only to peruse the *Tales of the Arabian Nights* or the fairy tales of Hans Christian Andersen or the Brothers Grimm to be reminded of how entertainment fantasy has always differed from idealized family life. Hansel and Gretel, for example, found themselves in the clutches of a witch because of an indifferent father and a cruel, selfish stepmother, and this primal childhood image long pre-dated the scapegoat decade of the Sixties! I think it may be worthwhile to re-think these dark myths—but such a process can only be useful if we recognize how deeply they tap into human consciousness, not if we glibly attack the latest messenger to bring us this ancient psychological news.

Every generation of kids is fascinated by sex and violence and the need to separate themselves from earlier generations. Long before electronic media existed, Mark Twain joked that "My father is so dumb, when I was eighteen I didn't speak to him until I was twenty-one. I was amazed at how much he had learned in those three years." One can deeply respect parents and parenting and still recognize the validity of a complex range of entertainments. One can also recognize the strange transition that parents go through from having recently been children and teenagers themselves to suddenly feeling the burdens of responsibility and the ticking clock of middle age. One can be horrified by teen-age violence, materialism, and other forms of immorality and yet still acknowledge that adult self-righteous resentment of youthful exuberance, rebellion, and folly is not always based on moral concerns.

The Dangerous Snobbishness of the Elite

Similarly there is a dangerous snobbishness that pervades elite culture bashing. It is not morally sufficient to simply describe popular entertainment as "poison," based on themes that are as prevalent in opera as they are in daytime soaps. If the murderous protagonists of Richard Wright's *Native Son* and [Fyodor] Dostoyevsky's *Crime and Punishment* are more morally framed than those of Master P. and Wu-Tang Clan, elite adult critics should be expected to explain why, not to simply deride modern popular music as garbage. After all, even if one assumes that Hewlett and West are right about every single work they attack, even if the motives of all creators and businesspeople involved with entertainment are totally selfish—there are tens of millions of fans who actually like what they see and hear. If they are to be educated, they first must be understood.

As for the proliferation of four-letter words, there is no doubt that Supreme Court decisions of the Sixties and Seventies decriminalized words that previously were the property of sports coaches and military commanders. Clearly different generations and social groups have their own taste and sensibilities about four-letter words, but mores and morals are not the same. Personally, I think that Eddie Cantor singing about "making whoopee," Jerry Lee Lewis shouting about "great balls of fire," the Beatles harmonizing "I wanna hold your hand," and Nine Inch Nails screaming "I want to fuck you like an animal" are all talking about the same thing.

I believe that the tragic deterioration of U.S. families in

recent years has almost nothing to do with entertainment. Canadian citizens receive virtually all of the same entertainment as we in the United States but, absent the devastating legacy of slavery and racism, and with different public policy—including public health care, better funded public schools, and far greater gun control—Canada has dramatically better statistics in terms of crime, child abuse, etc. Moreover, most art and entertainment have positive effects: creating a shared language, a sense of community, relieving stress, and making people feel less alone in the world.

No Evidence That Media Violence Causes Actual Violence

Would the incidence of violence, sex, and intoxication seriously diminish if those topics disappeared from our screens? That seems to be the apple-pie view of most psychologists. But it is not a point that has been proved. . . .

Professor Jonathan Freedman of the Department of Psychology at the University of Toronto reviewed the literature in 1984 and concluded that "there is little convincing evidence that in natural settings viewing television violence causes people to be more aggressive." In 1992, he wrote that "research has not produced the kind of strong, reliable, consistent results that we usually require to accept an effect as proved. It may be that watching violent programs causes increased aggressiveness, but from a scientific point of view, this has not been demonstrated. Our public statements should reflect this."

But suppose there was some direct relationship between popular entertainment and the apparent erosion of cultural values. What could we do about it in any public way? We could try to return to censorship. Some conservatives talk wistfully of the good old days of movie censorship. There would be legal hurdles, but perhaps not impossible ones.

But do we want broad censorship on sex and violence? How much good could it do? No, and not much.

Ben J. Wattenberg, *Values Matter Most*, 1995.

This is not to say that entertainment is a purely passive reflection of society. Obviously artists and the business people who give them access to electronic media make aesthetic and moral choices. But it is silly not to recognize that the majority of the content of public entertainment is driven by public taste and experience, and that the very evils that Hewlett and West document so eloquently elsewhere in *The War Against Parents* create the raw material for both the creation and consumption of depressing entertainment. Is it a coincidence that virtually all of the anti-police and "cop killer" rap lyrics of the 1980s came from young African American citizens of Los Angeles who grew up in a community dominated by a Daryl Gates-led LAPD?

Outrageous Claims About Media Violence

Violent entertainment is not, contrary to the hysterical ravings of anti-entertainment social scientists, anything like tobacco. Tobacco contains uniform chemical substances, the effects of which have been demonstrated in tests over decades on thousands of people. No two pieces of entertainment are the same. Reasonable people do not always agree on what violence is. Many pseudo-scientists who study media, counting "acts of violence," include cartoon and comic violence in their tallies. Hewlett and West make the outrageous claim that MTV music videos average twenty acts of violence per hour, and that sixty percent of programming on MTV links violence to degrading sexual portrayals. As someone who watches a lot of MTV and who submits music videos to them on a regular basis, I can say unequivocally that these statistics are grossly inaccurate. Because of the scrutiny they are under, MTV has more stringent standards limiting sex and violence than virtually any other entertainment medium. There is virtually nothing on the channel that depicts violence as explicitly as movies, network television, or literature. Sex on MTV is overwhelmingly, conventionally, (and non-violently) heterosexual and much less graphic than in other media. Aimed at teenagers and people in their early twenties, MTV videos can seem puerile to adults or to intellectual or iconoclastic kids. But it is wrong to confuse subjective aesthetic taste with objective morals.

Can there be a new progressive politics without the participation of young people and non-intellectuals? Do we want to force these constituencies to leave their enthusiasm for their culture at the door of politics? Will this help attract them?

The millions of people who like rap or Oliver Stone movies are not robots programmed at will by demonic entertainment business geniuses. Yes, the market mentality affects entertainment as it does every business (including academia), and greed far too often replaces morality. But the psychological and spiritual levers of change are as likely to be found in the imagination of artists and the inarticulate emotional response to them by various publics as they would in polemics.

A healthy respect for the nuances and context of entertainment culture can give rise to a moral influence from visionaries such as Hewlett and West—but to have credibility, they must be willing to look at culture with compassion and respect and not with ivory tower condescension.

| "When symbols of the sacred become nothing more than just another way to move . . . product, . . . we lose something important— the sense that some things are of enduring value, above the mundane world of buying or selling."

Advertising Demeans American Values

Marylaine Block

In the following viewpoint, Marylaine Block states that advertising cheapens American culture by teaching that nothing is too sacred to be used to sell a product. Furthermore, she contends, advertising glorifies antisocial behavior, promotes greed, and damages people's self-esteem. Block is a librarian and a columnist for *Fox News Online*.

As you read, consider the following questions:
1. What are the good qualities of advertising, as explained by the author?
2. In what ways do ads glorify lawlessness and abuse the sacred, in Block's view?
3. According to Block, how can individuals counter the harmfulness of advertising?

Excerpted from "Ad Lib," by Marylaine Block in her column, My Word's Worth, www.qconline.com/myword/ad.html, June 1996. Reprinted with permission from the author.

As I was driving to Michigan last week, a cute little tune kept circling around in my head, and I kept trying to figure out what it was—Tom Petty, maybe? No, though the voice sounded like his. And then it came to me. It was a jingle about a chemical that would kill all my corn bores (not a problem I actually have). If you live in Iowa and you watch the news, there's no way you're going to avoid knowing all kinds of advertising jingles for pesticides and fertilizers. They're such catchy tunes, and they sneak into your head whether you want them there or not. . . .

American culture is powerfully infiltrated and shaped by . . . commercials. There is a good side to this. An awful lot of our brightest, most creative artists, wordsmiths, filmmakers and composers go into advertising because there are a lot more jobs there than there are in feature films or television programs. As a consequence, a lot of the ads are funny, warm, even moving. Some of my favorite television moments are from ads. I remember fondly the commercial showing a little boy walking along, enticing a kitten by dropping bits of cat food, then crashing through his front door hollering, "Look what followed me home!" And the current McDonald's advertising campaign about future Olympians, such as the future discus thrower, a little girl throwing her plate off her high chair.

A Source of Cultural Knowledge

Ads are a rich source of shared cultural knowledge, because we all see the same ads, even if we don't necessarily see the same programs. We adopt tag lines from ads all the time: "The Pepsi generation." "Just do it." "I can't believe I ate the whole thing!" "Where's the beef?" Of course, simplicity like this doesn't come easy; some ad agency writer sweated blood to come up with these cute pithy sayings that resonate, that sum up a common public attitude. But once these sayings are in the marketplace, we appropriate them, because they are a valuable shorthand. The images that go with the words are another part of our shared knowledge, and the images are then played on by other advertisers, and other artists, such as Andy Warhol.

Ads are also little mini-dramas that, like any TV drama,

show us how to behave. If we have no other models of how to handle certain social situations, we can draw on the ads. The Tasters' Choice commercials (about a budding romance that began when one of them needed to borrow some coffee) offer a model of sophisticated courtship. Long-distance telephone ads and Folger's coffee ads offer wonderful models of family warmth and tenderness. And *lots* of ads offer models of flirtation. . . .

But the purpose of the ads is to sell, and that means that they need to appeal to us at gut level, overtly and subliminally. And this means that certain American values and attitudes are exaggerated almost to the point of lunacy.

Americans place an inordinate value on personal freedom. We value pristine wilderness. So the ads for jeeps and off-road vehicles tell us we can go wherever we want, roads or no roads; the images on the screen are of mountains and deserts and forests. Many of us know perfectly well that taking these vehicles into these fragile environments will cause untold damage to the delicate ecology, but the purpose of those images, and that music, and those emotive words is to bypass our reason and slip sideways into our brains.

Glorifying Lawlessness and Abusing the Sacred

In a number of recent commercials, that love of personal freedom has taken a further step into the actual glorification of lawlessness. "Break all the rules," we are told in a number of campaigns. The people who are shown abiding by normal social conventions are timid, dorky-looking people, that nobody in their right minds would try to emulate. The good-looking studs, the guys who are having all the fun, are the ones who are defying all the rules. (Of course they do this by buying, wearing, drinking, or eating, a product that anybody else can buy, wear, drink or eat.)

Just as our ads themselves provide quick, shorthand summations of cultural attitudes, so are the advertisers driven to use already existing cultural shorthand. The more expensive advertising time becomes, the shorter the ads get; the shorter the ads get, the less time they have to convey both information and emotive power.

This, I think, accounts for the way ads use and abuse symbols of the sacred. Teddy Roosevelt, on Mt. Rushmore, becomes a shill for toothpaste. Nuns and monks and Charlie Chaplin tell us what computers to buy. The statue of liberty sells underarm deodorant. The Beatles sing "Revolution" in order to sell athletic shoes. Cary Grant and Humphrey Bogart film clips are mutated into soft drink endorsements.

"Soul Shock" Advertising

"Soul shock" . . . ads aren't clever, or coy, so much as deeply unsettling. *Advertising Age* columnist Bob Garfield calls them "advertrocities." Examples? Benetton's dying AIDS patients and dead Bosnian soldiers. Calvin Klein models drowsing in shooting galleries with hunted, heroin-hollowed eyes. Recently the Italian jeansmaker Diesel launched an extremely disturbing print campaign. The company's cryptic ads-within-ads, set in North Korea, feature images of, for example, skinny models on the side of a bus packed with (presumably) starving, suffering locals. "There's no limit to how thin you can get," says the ad on the bus. . . .

"Soul shock" targets our values. There's probably something immoral about ads that inure people to the suffering of other people. The way shock encourages malaise reminds me of what David Korten called the "cycle of alienation," to which today's jaded consumers are somehow intuitively wise. [Basically, we move through four stations: (1) Advertisers assure us their products will make us whole. (2) Buying their product requires money. (3) The quest for money widens the gap between ourselves, family and community. (4) Deepening alienation creates a sense of social and spiritual emptiness, which can only be assuaged by . . . see (1).] The first time you see a starving child on late-night TV, you're appalled. You send money. But as these images become more familiar, your compassion fades. These ads start to repulse you. You never want to see a starving kid again. Cynical consumers understand what's being done to them. They just don't really care.

Bruce Grierson, *Adbusters*, Winter 1998.

When symbols of the sacred become nothing more than just another way to move the product, though, we lose something important—the sense that some things are of enduring value, above the mundane world of buying and selling.

Celebrities are also useful for the quick sell, because we recognize them, and associate certain values with them.

Michael Jordan: outstanding athleticism. Basketball player Dennis Rodman: flake. Indiana basketball coach Bobby Knight: throwing chairs when displeased with the referees or his players. It is unfortunate that commercials lately have been using some of the more antisocial characteristics of celebrities as jokes: Deion Sanders (football and baseball player) trading jokes with his team's owner about his exorbitant salary; Bobby Knight trying, not very successfully, to be easygoing when one of his players has done something stupid; Dennis Rodman refusing to do something because it's too wild and crazy.

The problem with this is that it treats these traits as if they're cute and endearing. Ugly temper tantrums, greed, craziness, are made to seem like perfectly acceptable behavior. "In your face" has become a bizarre sort of compliment. . . .

Our advertising has a mixed effect on us. It does have a uniting effect, in the sense that we all recognize and use the same advertising jokes and tag lines. The ads bring our values out into the open, though revealing them in a curious, funhouse mirror image. They show us idealized versions of ourselves: youthful, carefree, independent, daring, and above all, free.

Why Advertising Degrades American Values

But above all, our advertising cheapens and demeans our culture.

1. It tells us that no value, be it God or country or family, is too sacred to be put to use in selling a product.
2. It doesn't worry about the consequences of pushing our hot buttons, like personal freedom.
3. It doesn't worry about glorifying antisocial behavior.
4. It doesn't worry about the social consequences of fostering greed and a permanent sense of grievance because we never have quite enough stuff.
5. It doesn't care that showing only pretty people devalues ordinary-looking human beings.
6. It doesn't care that it's teaching children to want things and whine until they get them.
7. It doesn't worry about the consequences of telling us that politicians are just another product to be pushed.

There's not a whole lot that America, as a society, can do about this. Our television and radio have been run by advertisers from the very beginning, and we are all addicted to our "free" entertainment. Our current government is hostile to the notion of publicly funded broadcasting, and public TV doesn't compete all that well against the commercial networks in any case. Commercials are our past, our present, and our future.

But as individuals, we have these powers:

1. We can recognize what ads are doing to us.
2. We can turn the damn things off. It may be that God gave us the remote control for a good reason.
3. We can refuse to buy the product.
4. We can tell the advertisers why we will not buy the product.
5. We can tell them that some things are sacred, and if they abuse the sacred they will lose us as customers.
6. We can tell them that we are a better people than they think we are, and better than they portray us in their ads.

| *"Advertising represents the triumph of the consumer over the power of producers and vested interests."*

Advertising Is Important to Consumers

John Hood

In the subsequent viewpoint, John Hood asserts that advertising is an essential and valuable element of a free society. Because ads convey crucial information about the price, quality, and availability of products, they save consumers time and energy. In addition, Hood argues, advertising images are responsible for part of the pleasure people take in making purchases. Hood is president of the John Locke Foundation, a think tank based in North Carolina, and the author of *The Heroic Enterprise: Business and the Common Good.*

As you read, consider the following questions:

1. What common criticisms of advertising does Hood mention?
2. How does advertising help alleviate the obvious dilemma that consumers face every day?
3. How does advertising help create meaning and enjoyment in people's lives?

Excerpted from "In Praise of Advertising," by John Hood, *Consumers Research Magazine*, April 1, 1998. Reprinted with the permission of *Consumers Research Magazine*.

For the last few years—until 1998, at least—the Super Bowl hasn't exactly featured the most interesting and competitive of football games. They've been blowouts, over by the first half at the latest. But one form of competition has remained as strong and vibrant as ever: the fight to put on the most memorable television advertisement. Over the years, many such ads have made their debut during the Super Bowl, including Apple's "1984" ads touting their new Macintosh, celebrity ads for Pepsi and Coke, and the croaking frogs of "Bud-wei-ser."

Isn't there something wrong with this picture? Should advertising overshadow that for which it is supposed to be merely a sponsor? Well, the answers to these questions lie far beyond the game of football. As James Twitchell, author of *Adcult USA: The Triumph of Advertising in American Culture* points out, it isn't just the Super Bowl ads that live on long after the game is forgotten. Advertising generates powerful and lasting social symbols. Think of Morris the cat, Mikey the Life cereal kid, the Marlboro Man, the Jolly Green Giant, the Energizer Bunny. Think of tunes like "I'd Like to Teach the World to Sing," "Plop, Plop, Fizz, Fizz," and "We've Only Just Begun" (a song the Carpenters made a hit after it had already been widely heard in a bank commercial). Think of slogans like "Have it your way," "Just do it," "Snap, crackle, pop," and "Be all you can be."

The ubiquity of advertising, as well as its apparent excess and wastefulness, has led many social critics and would-be consumer "advocates" to demonize it. "Advertising is the science of arresting the human intelligence long enough to get money from it," wrote one critic. Novelist George Orwell said advertising "is the rattling of a stick inside a swill bucket." Clare Boothe Luce wrote that advertising had "done more to cause the social unrest of the twentieth century than any other single factor." A common attack is that ads manufacture consumers' demand for products that they would otherwise not feel a need to buy. "Few people at the beginning of the nineteenth century needed an adman to tell them what they wanted," groused economist John Kenneth Galbraith.

"The institutions of modern advertising and salesmanship," he continued, ". . . cannot be reconciled with the notion of independently determined desires, for their central function is to create desires—to bring into being wants that previously did not exist."

But there is another side to advertising, one that these and other social commentators have largely overlooked. Advertising represents the triumph of the consumer over the power of producers and vested interests. Commercial advertising, at least, is found only in societies where individuals have the right to choose their own goods and services from competing suppliers. Ads convey critical information about price, quality, and availability. Furthermore, in many cases ads are indistinguishable from the product; to consume it is to express yourself through the symbols that ads have invoked (the thrill of driving a new car down a highway is a good example of this phenomenon).

In short, advertising is good for consumers. It's worth exploring how in greater detail.

The Economics of Advertising

Many of advertising's critics have portrayed it as playing either no role or a counterproductive role in advancing consumer interests. For example, some economists have long argued that ads create barriers to entry in particular industries, thus reducing competition and making prices higher. This happens, it is argued, because the ads differentiate an existing product—say, a breakfast cereal—from a possible competing product that might taste better or cost less, or both. Consumers might be better off trying this new product, but they are already made familiar with the existing product's name through ads and thus don't make the buying decision that would best satisfy their wants.

This model of consumer decision-making neglects to address an obvious dilemma that all of us face every day: limited time and attention span. Given the multitude of activities each of us carries out every day, it is a myth to suggest that we have the time, ability, or inclination to gather perfect information about every alternative available for every good or service we wish to purchase. Because of this practical constraint on market decisions, clever and memorable advertising serves a useful function if it establishes loyalty to a brand that offers us what we want. Of course, advertising alone won't create a lasting attachment. We have to experience the good, and actually enjoy it or find it beneficial and economical. Once having done so, however, brand loyalty then helps us remember and subsequently purchase that useful good again without having to spend a great deal of costly time and resources searching for it.

One study of brand loyalty did, indeed, find that for consumer products such as soft drinks, electric shavers, hair spray, detergents, and cigarettes, consumers do display a kind of brand loyalty called "inertia." That is, they tend to buy the same brand consistently. But as economists Robert B. Ekelund, Jr. and David S. Saurman wrote in their award-wining book *Advertising and the Market Process*, "to conclude that advertising of these brands cause the inertia would be similar to convicting a suspect with only the prosecutor's opening statement to the jury as evidence."

In fact, one obvious reason why some products that are bought often tend to display consumer inertia is that consumers are well-satisfied with them, and have made the rational judgment that alternative products are unlikely to provide significantly better value. More important, Ekelund and Saurman report that the intensity of advertising more often correlates with less consumer inertia rather than more. Expenditures are higher, in other words, where consumers exhibit less clear attachment to one brand. Another study found that, from 1948 to 1959, the market share of leading brands actually decreased in highly advertised industries; indeed, the market share of leading brands in toiletries and cosmetics, the highest-advertised industry in the study, decreased faster than in industries such as soap and food, where advertising expenditures were lower.

Advertising Encourages Competition

More generally, Ekelund and Saurman report that competition among firms is, if anything, more fierce—and market shares more uncertain—in industries with higher-than-average advertising expenditures. "The more intensively all firms in industries advertise," they write, "the less stable are market shares or the more these market shares tend to change." The reason is obvious. It's not just the market leaders who get to advertise. So do their rivals. For entrants into a new sector, advertising isn't a barrier but an opportunity. How else can a new producer get the attention of a busy consumer, and get him or her to try something new? Advertising, far from being a constraint on vigorous competition, is more likely a necessary prerequisite for it to occur.

The Attraction of Things

Human beings like things. We buy things. We like to exchange things. We steal things. We donate things. We live through things. We call these things "goods," as in "goods and services." We do not call them "bads.". . . The still-going-strong Industrial Revolution produces more and more things, not because production is what machines do, and not because nasty capitalists twist their handlebar mustaches and mutter, "More slop for the pigs," but because we are powerfully attracted to the world of things. Advertising, when it's lucky, supercharges some of this attraction.

James B. Twitchell, *Wilson Quarterly*, Summer 1996.

What about prices? Surely, one might surmise, the hundreds of billions of dollars a year spent on intensive advertising are passed along, at least in part, to consumers in the form of higher prices. But this view is completely contradicted by the facts. Take eyeglasses. For years, some states restricted or banned advertising for eye examinations and eyeglasses, while others did not. This gave researchers a good data set from which to draw conclusions about advertising and price. As it turns out, states that limited advertising had eyeglass prices that were 25% higher than their peers without ad restrictions. To take the most extreme examples, Washington, D.C. and Texas had no advertising restrictions at all, while North Carolina had the most wide-ranging restrictions in the nation. North Carolina eyeglass prices were double those in D.C. and Texas.

Another study looked at gasoline prices. After adjusting for income and other factors, American Enterprise Institute researchers Thom Kelly and Alex Maurizi found that regions where gas stations displayed their prices prominently to drivers had significantly lower average gas prices than regions where the prices, for whatever reason, weren't clearly visible from the road. Interestingly, this study not only demonstrated how advertising can reduce prices by encouraging competition, but did so with billboard advertising—one of the most loathed forms of commercial activity on the part of many critics.

Finally, the relationship between advertising and product quality deserves a mention. It appears to be strongest for products that are expensive and purchased infrequently. For disposable "experience goods" like soap or food that are purchased often, consumers develop their own body of information about quality. They either like a brand or they don't. But for high-cost, high-value "search goods" such as automobiles, farm equipment, computers, or household appliances, consumers seem to demand information on quality. One study of the Yellow Pages bore this out. Ads for search goods and services were four to 12 times more likely to include information about licensing or certification, consumer ratings, and other quality selling points than did ads for experience goods, which focused more on price and availability.

Advertising and Desire

Some critics of advertising grant that it plays an important role in the competitive process, but still criticize it for "creating" consumer demand where it would otherwise not exist. In particular, many point to advertising for products such as perfumes and soft drinks that rely rarely on price or specific quality information and more on images, music, celebrities, or symbolism. What practical benefit could this kind of advertising possibly provide? Isn't it just an expensive and wasteful form of brain candy?

Only if one adopts a limited, even soulless, view of markets. After all, they don't exist simply to supply proteins, mildly stimulative liquid refreshments, tonal recreational amenities, or person-carrying devices. They give us sizzling steaks, a beer after work, a concert on Saturday night, and a fast car to get us there. As in other areas of our lives—such as family or faith—free enterprise is a means by which we seek meaning and enjoyment. The extent to which advertising contributes to that function is greater than is usually perceived.

Take sports merchandise. No matter how many Nike shorts or Air Jordans you wear, you are very unlikely to be as good at basketball as the athletes who advertise these wares. No matter how many banners, jackets, buttons, or flags you buy with your favorite team's logo on them, you will never actually be part of the team or directly share in its wins or losses. But that isn't the point. People seem to enjoy expressing their affinity, their affection for their heroes and teams by sporting their colors. It makes the game more meaningful to them.

Similarly, the fact that millions of Americans are buying four-wheel-drive sport-utility vehicles will not change the fact that most will never actually use them as some of the people in ads do—to haul things, for example, or to go four-wheeling through rugged mountain terrain. Even images of families with children heading home from soccer practice don't necessarily comport with the actual use of sport utilities by young singles. But something about those images resonates with the buyer. It might be a true aspiration to do those things, or just a sense that the purchase of such a vehicle might expand their possibilities. Whatever the source, it is obvious that in these cases the advertising becomes, in a way, part of the good being purchased. To some extent, the buyer of a new Mustang convertible is buying the feeling that ads for the convertible have expressed, a sense of freedom or adventure.

The Virtue of Advertising

Some may view this side of advertising as a vice, but I see it as a virtue. It doesn't mean that advertising actually creates a demand for a product. It's not that powerful. The desire for goods and services to make our lives safer, cleaner, easier, and more enjoyable is already implanted deep within us. What advertising does is merely to bring that desire out into the open, and give it a distinct form. As James Twitchell observes, "the real work of Madison Avenue is not to manipulate the doltish public but to find out how people already live . . . not to make myth but to make your product part of an already existing code." He summarizes the concept neatly this way:

"Advertising is simply one of a number of attempts to load objects with meaning. It is not a mirror, a lamp, a magnifying glass, a distorted prism, a window, a trompe l'oeil, or a subliminal embedment as much as it is an ongoing conversation within a culture about the meanings of objects. It does not follow or lead so much as it interacts. Advertising is neither chicken nor egg. Let's split the difference, it's both. It is language not just about objects to be consumed but about the consumers of objects."

It is also a language that is spoken only in a society where individuals—not guilds, not bureaucracies, not all-powerful institutions—ultimately decide what goods and services will be produced and consumed. They do so by exercising their choice as consumers. Advertising helps them do that. It's no more complicated than that.

Periodical Bibliography

The following articles have been selected to supplement the diverse views presented in this chapter. Addresses are provided for periodicals not indexed in the *Readers' Guide to Periodical Literature*, the *Alternative Press Index*, the *Social Sciences Index*, or the *Index to Legal Periodicals and Books*.

Holly Lyman Antolini — "Naming Our Demons," *The Witness*, April 1999. Available from 7000 Michigan Ave., Detroit, MI 48210-2872.

Jeff Cohen — "In Hot Pursuit—or in Heat?" *Extra!* March/April 1998. Available from 130 West 25th St., New York, NY 10001.

Todd Gitlin — "The Culture of Celebrity," *Dissent*, Summer 1998. Available from the Foundation for the Study of Independent Social Ideas, Inc., 521 Fifth Ave., Suite 1700, New York, NY 10017.

Adam Gopnick — "Culture Vultures," *New Yorker*, May 24, 1999.

Cynthia Grenier — "TV: Getting Down and Dirty," *World & I*, August 1998. Available from 3400 New York Ave. NE, Washington, DC 20002.

William F. Jasper — "Lessons From Columbine High," *New American*, June 7, 1999. Available from 770 Westhill Blvd., Appleton, WI 54914.

Thomas L. Jipping — "Diagnosing the Cultural Virus," *World & I*, July 1999.

John Leo — "When Life Imitates Video," *U.S. News & World Report*, May 3, 1999.

Michael Medved — "Hollywood Murdered Innocence," *Wall Street Journal*, June 16, 1999.

Peggy Noonan — "The Culture of Death," *Wall Street Journal*, April 22, 1999.

Mary Pipher — "Surviving Toxic Media: How the Church Can Help," *World*, January/February 1998. Available from Unitarian Universalist Association, 25 Beacon St., Boston, MA 02108-2803.

Terry Teachout — "The Unreal Presence," *Crisis*, June 1999.

Karl Zinsmeister — "TV-Free: Real Families Describe Life Without the Tube," *American Enterprise*, September/October 1997. Available from American Enterprise Institute for Public Policy Research, 1150 17th NW, Washington, DC 20036.

CHAPTER 4

What Measures Would Improve American Values?

Chapter Preface

It was less than thirty years ago that American society referred to illegitimate children as "bastards," promiscuous women as "sluts," and homeless people as "bums." Such labels are less commonly used today because they are considered derogatory. However, according to some modern-day critics, derogatory labels are one of the chief ways that society discourages destructive behavior. In the view of these critics, the shame associated with being called a drunk, for example, is powerful enough to deter people from excessive drinking.

Many of those who feel America is in moral decline believe that society would benefit from a renewal of public shame. As columnists Jonathan Alter and Pat Wingert write, "Properly calibrated, shame falls somewhere between mild embarrassment and cruel humiliation. The goal is not mere retribution but conformity—good conformity, the kind that makes it easier for people to form communities."

However, other commentators warn that reinstating social taboos would be dangerous. They argue that societal shame would unfairly punish people whose behavior does not conform to rigid norms set down by the majority. These commentators question whether America was really better off in the days when pregnant teens were forced to drop out of school and alcoholics were considered "sinners."

Other observers doubt whether negative stigmas actually prevent bad behavior. Professor of psychology June Tagney says that rather than encouraging rehabilitation, shame causes people to "withdraw and deny responsibility [for their actions]." In Tagney's opinion, "When people are shamed, they're not terribly motivated to change their behavior, and they often do the opposite."

Although legislators on both sides of the political spectrum have debated the need for social stigmas, whether or not shame makes a comeback ultimately depends upon the values of society. While some believe that social norms are the best way to improve morality in America, others argue that individual responsibility, legislation, or character education are more effective approaches. Authors debate these issues in the following chapter.

"The only way [America's problems] will be solved is if certain people feel bad—not that they go to jail, pay a fine, do community service, but that they feel *bad."*

Shame Deters Immoral Behavior

James B. Twitchell

In the following viewpoint, James B. Twitchell explains the benefits of shame on society. According to Twitchell, the shaming of immoral or destructive behavior provides a strong incentive for people to avoid such behavior. Twitchell is a professor of English at the University of Florida at Gainesville, and the author of *Lead Us Into Temptation* and *For Shame: The Loss of Common Decency in American Culture*, from which this viewpoint has been excerpted.

As you read, consider the following questions:
1. In Twitchell's view, how should society apply shame to the issue of reproductive habits?
2. What changes does the author recommend in education policies?
3. How can ostracism be beneficial, in the author's view?

Excerpted from *For Shame: The Loss of Common Decency in American Culture*, by James B. Twitchell. Copyright ©1997 by James B. Twitchell. Reprinted with the permission of St. Martin's Press, LLC.

Clearly human biology and evolution have hardwired us to experience the jolt of shame for a purpose. Shame shocks in every culture, and in every culture this frisson is painful—especially to the young. Although the sensation may be pan-cultural, individual cultures write the operating instructions for these shame programs, and they can inscribe wildly different protocols. Sometimes the codes appear to make no sense whatsoever. They often seem gibberish from both inside and outside a culture. Why can't I say that word? It's just a bunch of phonemes. The very illogic of much shame may account for part of its power. Give up personal control, it demands, do this, don't question it, don't do that, get in line, conform. The lesson from history is not so much what lasting cultures forbid as it is that they forbid certain acts and then apply shame continually and fairly to the violators.

The Power of Shame

In other words, if the jolt of shame is used to encourage co-operation—regardless of the task at hand—it produces a sense of community and hence stability. The group can now get on to matters of more import; the bond has been made. However, if shaming is used to intimidate and exclude legitimate members of the society, then it only undermines the sense of unity. Shame becomes not unifying but fractious. Tell the "haves" they can behave one way, tell the "have-nots" they must behave differently, and trouble is on the way. You can set your watch by it. The dustbin of history is filled with such erstwhile cultures and has room for plenty more.

Knowing this, we might do well to consider that shame is no enemy and shamelessness no friend. The object is not to be free of shame but to be ashamed of behavior that is dangerous to the community. In fact, we might do well to admit that using shame is nothing to be ashamed of; rather, it shows an understanding that feeling bad often has a central purpose. Using shame to oppress, however, is not only cruel but ultimately counterproductive.

We had better learn how to invoke shame, because so many of our current problems can't be solved by clicking the remote control. The only way they will be solved is if certain people feel bad—not that they go to jail, pay a fine, do community service, but that they *feel* bad. When they break a code, they need to feel a hot blush passing over their faces. In a weird kind of homeopathic voodoo, they need to feel a little death lest a bigger one ensue.

Since the relatively recent replacement of a hierarchical culture, controlled from above, with a carnival culture, controlled from below, our temptation has been to think that feeling bad is just not "right." Bad feelings, we think, must be a sign of some disturbance, some churning of otherwise still waters, some flaw in the personality or in a relationship. Losing face hurts and it is often not fair. In our typically adolescent response to painful anxiety, we say to the shamer, "Don't be a downer. Quit laying this trip on me. Leave me alone. Don't pass judgment." This is the language of child to parent, and it has become the baby boomer's lingua franca. I'm okay, you're okay, we're okay. We rarely consider that feeling bad, feeling the blush of shame, may indeed be culture's way, the family's way, and even the individual's way of maintaining social balance and purpose. Sometimes you are not okay. Me too.

For instance, here are some problems for which public policies must depend on shame to succeed. In each case, since the 1960s, our well-intentioned but overly solicitous government has done just the opposite. Shame has been effectively removed as the feds have come in to pay the short-term price.

How Society Can Apply Shame

• *Population:* We need to make people feel very bad for careless reproduction habits. You certainly don't need to call the offspring bastards, but you should consider calling *both* parents something derogatory regardless of race, sex, or class. In the antediluvian days of my youth, pregnant teens were placed in special classes or schools. This raised the ire of many who thought this was discriminatory. It was. The government has since insisted that unwed mothers be "mainstreamed" or else the schools would be prohibited from receiving federal funds. Ask teenage girls today if they would consider having a baby out of wedlock and 55 percent say they would. Why not put the unwed fathers in special classes? Someone should be discriminated against. Illegitimacy should not be considered a birthright. If we are as concerned about child abuse as we claim, then we might consider that giving subsidies (about half of all AFDC [Aid to Families with Dependent Children] spending goes to families formed by unwed teens) and special legal protection to children having children is a particularly virulent (because it seems so compassionate) form of mistreating our children.

Shame Reinforces Moral Standards

Not so long ago, the English language featured an extensive lexicon of epithets that expressed disgust for miscreants who dared to break the rules or challenge social conventions.

If you were a guy who made ill use of a woman, people would dismiss you as a rake, a Lothario, bounder or cad.

Women of ill repute got such scarlet labels as tart, trollop or strumpet; chippie, hussy or heterae; Jezebel, floozy or home-wrecker.

People used these words in actual conversations, with the aim of discouraging bad behavior and reinforcing standards essential for maintaining civil society.

Tony Snow, *Conservative Chronicle*, November 5, 1997.

• *Violence:* We need to make the use of force into something shameful. When gunfire is the second leading cause of death among Americans ages ten to nineteen, you know that the codes of repression have unraveled early. Perhaps in addition to the V-chip, which will shunt violent programming past the impressionable young, we need an S-chip to do just the opposite with shame. A great deal of Western literature does precisely that. We had best not lose it.

• *Education:* A series of level playing fields is necessary for an equitable society. School is one of them. Schools are not where noble social experiments take place, nor are they places to redress wrongs committed elsewhere. They are rooms in which fundamental skills necessary to make one's way to a better future are taught. You don't go to school to feel good, nor to be warehoused. You go into those rooms to learn how to read, write, do math, and think clearly. The lower grades should be funded the way we fund prestigious universities: overpay and underwork teachers. Then get out of the way. Shutter all graduate schools of education. Quarantine all their graduates. My worst students go into K–12 teaching: that's shameful. My best go to law school; that's even worse. Ironically, many of the budding law students would much prefer to go into teaching, but that job has been made intolerable by low pay, lower prestige, a bingo curriculum, wacky administrators, and incessant government meddling. Few adolescents need a Harvard education, but every child should have a public Phillips Andover [a prestigious private school] available.

• *Race and gender:* We need to make such well-meaning but ill-conceived programs as race norming, affirmative action, minority set-asides, and quotas shameful (to many they already are) by providing equitable rewards for hard work, and special help for the genuinely disadvantaged.

• *Addiction:* We need to quit explaining bad habits in terms of chemical or genetic addictions. You should be ashamed of being an alcoholic even if your genes "predispose" you to drink too much. Willpower trumps predilection. The current vogue of "medicalizing character" undermines our sense of personal responsibility and shame.

• *Values:* Evil is not relative, the Devil is not just a misunderstood fellow, Jesus was not a matinee idol, certain principles are better than others, and some are downright shameful.

Bringing Back Shame

But how do we do this? One thing is to bring back the penalty of public shame, namely, shunning. This is a legitimate part of our Western heritage. The Puritans did it. The Quakers did it. We do it during war. It used to be a major part of education. Not every problem has a legislative or judicial solution. Way back when, this was effective: Socrates chose death over shunning by his beloved Atheneans. Michael Milken feels worse losing his seat on the stock exchange than in doing jail time. Joe Six-pack, dumped by the Elks, is distraught. Deadbeat Dad doesn't want his neighbors to know about his callous behavior, let alone his kids. A gang member "dissed" in Harlem feels it too.

Ostracism—expulsion from the group—can be harsh on

the individual but beneficial to the group. It works best when loss of status can be easily observed by peers. Wherever you find an ideal of respectability, however dim, you find sensitivity to shame. Ironically, having the law send certain lawbreakers off to jail can be counter-productive when incarceration carries no humiliation. All too often, jail time has become the enemy of shame rather than its ally. Some debts are not so easily (and privately) paid. So, too, having public programs to remedy problems individuals must confront removes stigmas that ought to be applied not just for the individual but for the group. How else do the young learn responsible behavior? Welfare, as Charles Murray has argued in *Losing Ground*, can become "insidious" when it protects recipients—and onlookers—from the results of shameful actions. Reticence, a crucial component of social responsibility, is very often based on the fear of feeling shame. Very often that fear is acquired secondhand by watching others suffer.

We don't need to force adulterers to wear a scarlet letter, but it wouldn't hurt to send a stronger signal that such dangerous and reckless behavior is more than . . . inappropriate. We can't condemn illegitimacy while condoning divorce in families with young children. We can't control the shameless content of much television entertainment, but we can embarrass the advertisers who sponsor it. While Madonna may be oblivious to the danger of flaunting single parenthood, Gerald Levin, CEO of Time Warner, who writes some of her checks, is not. No one wants to get into the classroom, but it does no harm to remind instructors that no one is helped when all students get A's, or when poor students are simply passed on to graduation rather than held back to learn. Ministers can be praised for matters other than gathering a large flock and building bigger buildings. Psychologists and social workers who pride themselves on always supporting their "clients" regardless of the damage done to others might rethink their positions. They may have profited from the shame-removal industry, but have the rest of us? The feisty Laura Schlessinger, of the *Ask Dr. Laura* radio show, should not be the only counselor willing to discuss publicly the redemptive powers of shame. And, finally, while we can't make parents of youngsters stay together, we can hold them publicly accountable for the damage caused to their offspring.

Shame as Education

If we are going to speak the language of morality, we are going to have to use the S-word not on the distant others, but on the group near at hand. On us. We need to let the sensation do its work, even if it feels bad. We need to be willing to say, "Shame on you" to miscreants; to "put to shame" those who act carelessly; to criticize those who "know no shame"; and to say, "I'm sorry, I'm ashamed of myself" when we are wrong. Being "for shame" means being intolerant of behaviors that ultimately injure us all. Restoring shame requires not just being judgmental, but being willing to articulate that judgment to those who may simply not know how irresponsible they are being. We need always to remember, however, that the goal is not to shun but to educate. The final emphasis must always be on reintegration.

Most of all we need to quit being so frightened and ashamed of shame. It holds a central position in all lasting cultures for a reason. Shame is not the disease; properly used, it is the cure. As a social construction, it is how we communicate certain key virtues, how a sense of decency is developed. We are not born with an on-board governor of actions; morality has to be installed. Conformity to certain baseline standards is not a luxury, but a necessity. Like it or not, inflicting the sting of shame is how successful cultures have protected the group from the dangers of individual excess. Feeling bad is often the basis of a general good. Civilization is not without its discontents. The alternative is, as the Victorians knew and we have recently forgotten, worse, much worse.

| *"[Shame] leads to, and reinforces, censorship."*

Shame Is a Form of Censorship

Carl F. Horowitz

Carl F. Horowitz, Washington correspondent for *Investor's Business Daily*, argues in the subsequent viewpoint that the crusade to deter immoral behavior with shame threatens the freedom of Americans. Shaming is ultimately a form of censorship, contends Horowitz, because it insists that people conform to the "social mandates" of the majority or else be ostracized.

As you read, consider the following questions:
1. According to Horowitz, what is private censorship, and why is it harmful?
2. How does psychologist Robert Karn define a "shameful" person, as cited by the author?
3. In Horowitz's view, how does shame lead to and reinforce censorship?

Excerpted from "The Shaming Sham," by Carl F. Horowitz, *The American Prospect*, vol. 3, March/April 1997. Copyright ©1997 by The American Prospect. Reprinted with the permission of the author and *The American Prospect*.

"**P**unishment, ostracism, humiliation," thundered Tory essayist and avowed high-cholesterol gourmand Digby Anderson, slamming his fist onto the table. It was an unusual discussion panel I had stumbled upon at the Sheraton Washington Hotel in March 1994. National Review Institute, the in-house think tank of conservatism's flagship periodical, was holding a summit conference on "Challenges to Conservatism," and this panel held forth on the ailments of modern culture. English conservatives, like their American brethren, apparently see little but ailments. Anderson, the founder of the Social Affairs Unit, a London-based research institute, was certain he had the cure.

He would publish his bile the following year as part of a collection he edited for *National Review*'s press. Titled *This Will Hurt: The Restoration of Virtue and Civic Order*, the book's brutally proscriptive tone, its chillingly precise descriptions of how to deal with violators of proper social order, suggested an eighties-era *Saturday Night Live* skit, "The Anal Retentive Chef." But even a parody could not come up with chapters like "Administering Punishment Morally, Publicly, and Without Excuse," "Uniformity, Uniforms, and the Maintenance of Adult Authority," and "Ostracism and Disgrace in the Maintenance of a Precarious Social Order." Gertrude Himmelfarb's preface set the tone: "It is evident that we are suffering from a grievous moral disorder. . . . And that moral pathology requires strenuous moral purgatives and restoratives."

American acolytes of such collectivist tough love might not recommend to the decadent West the strategy of Afghanistan's theocratic government, where adulterers face a public execution by stoning in a mosque courtyard. Still, Senator Wayne Allard, Colorado Republican, who favors public hangings as a deterrent to street crime, wouldn't feel that to be completely out of place. Neither would former Education Secretary William Bennett, who once said he is not "morally opposed" to public beheadings of convicted drug dealers.

Taking Liberties with Liberty

Having lost the battles for government censorship, conservatives had to find some other way to stigmatize cultural enemies into feckless mush. Enter moral censorship, the New Ostracism, or simply, shame. It's the preferable alternative to official censorship, and it works—or, at least, that's what its champions would have the public believe. Candidate Bob Dole frequently called upon filmmakers and television producers to feel a "decent sense of shame"; popular conservative author and socialite Arianna Huffington coined the term "shamership" for precisely this end; *Newsweek* devoted its February 6, 1995, cover story to the subject of "shame."

By now the charges have hardened into editorial cant. Our culture is "coarsened." Hollywood and other media messengers are bombarding Americans with gratuitous sex and violence. The nuclear family is an endangered species. "Increasingly . . . individualism has gone awry, veering from self-reliance to self-indulgence," writes columnist Jay Ambrose. "Some Americans, it sometimes seems, can't differentiate liberty from libertinism." A certain desperation seems to have set in among these social critics. In its November issue, the conservative magazine *First Things* sponsored a symposium that included such luminaries as Robert Bork and Charles Colson. The theme was that America, long in the hands of alien forces within, may be so far gone as to require a revolution. Colson prayed it would not have to be violent—a sign, perhaps, that his Watergate days are not quite fully behind him.

The principal tool of their revolution is shame, for little else has sufficed. . . . A reduced welfare state, while desirable, won't deter the wealthy Unassimilated Other ("Hollywood") who don't need welfare in the first place. Philanthropy, even if guided by conservatives, can withhold, but cannot punish. Legal censorship, though needed in measured doses, is not feasible. Short of violence, shame is the best way to control errant behavior. "Where shame recovers vitality, the fear of shame can be a regulator of social conduct," wrote Michigan State University political philosopher William Allen in *This Will Hurt*.

But here's the rub: Shame is an expression of collective will. It is not simple opposition, however vociferous, to someone who is objectionable. Author P.J. O'Rourke, with his periodic (and not quite entirely facetious) Enemies Lists, may seek to stigmatize those dreaded Birkenstock-wearing liberals who eat low-calorie yogurt and listen to National Public Radio. But as a muckraker, he needs some heavy-duty help. Shame enables communities to let oddballs know there is nowhere to run or hide. That means, by extension, each member not only must avoid shameful behavior, but also must join the ritual punishment of offenders. In a culture war, slackers need not apply. The challenge is to find people—moral censors—with the will to lead such efforts.

Shame Versus Guilt

Experts say people should rightly feel guilty when they do something bad, but shame can actually cause people to do the very things shaming them is supposed to get them to avoid.

Michael Lewis, a Rutgers University professor of pediatrics and psychiatry and author of *Shame, The Exposed Self*, uses the example of a student failing a test to explain the difference. A student who fails and blames it on himself is experiencing shame, whereas one who focuses on the reasons why he did not pass, like not studying hard enough, is experiencing guilt. Shame is overwhelming and defeating whereas guilt can help a person change behavior for the better.

Peggy O'Crowley, *The Record*, March 17, 1996.

Censors everywhere take an interest in culture mainly to rid every medium of expressions of immodesty. Today's censors are as clueless as their ancestors, save for their application of a faux-scientific "content analysis" better suited to the news than to the arts. Roughly speaking, that means conservative researchers train and pay people to watch television, and tote up the number of positive and negative references to the family, capitalism, and the military on ten randomly selected episodes of the *The Simpsons*. That way, L. Brent Bozell, III, chairman of the conservative watchdog group the Media Research Center, can throw red meat to activists and grouse: "During the so-called family hour, the depictions of sex outside of marriage outnumber those of it within marriage by a factor of 8 to 1." This is the sort of arid "cultural" perspective that cares not a whit for films with Woody Allen or Hugh Grant but very much about their stars' insufficient repentance for offscreen peccadilloes, always with the tantalizing possibility of driving them out of work. . . .

Shaming Crusades

While pledging all due allegiance to the Bill of Rights, the new moral crusaders say that fear of ostracism, blacklisting, or a boycott is an efficient, "market-based" prod for self-policing within the artistic community. (How convenient that the free market and moral righteousness should be mutually reinforcing!) John Hood, president of the John Locke Foundation, a think tank based in Raleigh, North Carolina, offered the following defense of William Bennett and Charlton Heston's (successful) campaign to shame Time Warner into selling its stake in the perfidious Interscope Records: "Bennett and Heston never called for government action. Their chosen means of affecting corporate decision making were boycott threats and public shaming, both perfectly acceptable modes of discourse in a free society," he wrote in the July 1996 issue of *Reason* magazine.

Conservatives don't have the monopoly on this kind of thinking. Even generally liberal (or at least neoliberal) commentators like Jonathan Alter, writing in a recent issue of *Newsweek*, would have us believe there is a nice, clean philosophical line separating the censorship practiced by government through law and the censorship practiced by the private sector. Writes Alter: "Wal-Mart is not saying you can't make a CD full of explicit sex or gangster garbage; it's simply saying Wal-Mart won't sell it. Huge difference." The argument that groups acting outside of the political system have the right to set standards for decency and appropriate behavior also finds a voice in the communitarian movement, whose advocates include scholars (such as Michael Sandel) and political intellectuals (such as Amitai Etzioni) most observers would describe as progressive.

Yet private censorship doesn't look so harmless when you start to apply it. Sure, reflexive boycotts and shaming crusades by committees of cut-rate Comstocks [censors] technically fall within the realm of free speech. But moral censorship has a capacity to intrude upon a person's privacy that no bureaucracy, federal or otherwise, can match. John Stuart

Mill recognized more than a century ago why morally mobilized citizens, on the lookout for enemies, are society's ultimate censors. The informal social mandate, he observed, "practices a social tyranny more formidable than many kinds of political oppression, since, though not usually upheld by such extreme penalties, it leaves fewer means of escape, penetrating much more deeply into the details of life, and enslaving the soul itself." Protection against the tyranny of the magistrate would not be enough. Needed as well would be protection against "the tyranny of the prevailing opinion and feeling" that, as its goal, would "compel all characters to fashion themselves upon the model of its own."

Breaking the Nonconformist's Spirit

Filmmaker Oliver Stone, a bête noire of America's shamers, knows this. He has pointed out, rightly, that shaming at heart is McCarthyist. Senator Joe McCarthy never disavowed the First Amendment; he instead favored bullying political and cultural enemies into "behaving," or, failing that, he drove them out of work. That's the main idea behind shaming in any era: to break the nonconformist's spirit, instill in him self-loathing, and induce him to turn on his former comrades-in-arms. A "shameful" person is less a criminal than one who hasn't cooperated with his putative moral betters, as clinical psychologist Robert Karen notes. "(S)hame itself is less clearly about morality than about conformity, acceptability, or character. To be ashamed is to expect rejection, not so much of what one has done as because of what one is," he writes. Rabbi Daniel Lapin, writing in *This Will Hurt*, argues for shaming illegitimate children, surely a grotesque example of applying scarlet letters to social status rather than behavior.

Never mind that the cultural conservatives say it takes Mom and Dad, not a village, to raise a child—they're interested in the village too. University of Houston political scientist Ross Lence, in *This Will Hurt*, argues that families have broken down because modern cities cannot provide the reputation-shattering gossip found in smaller communities. Can suburbs, at least, create a healthy moral climate? Probably not, argues Karl Zinsmeister, writing in the November-December 1996 issue of the *American Enterprise*, because their physical design precludes vigilant neighbors from act-ing in loco parentis. "In traditional communities," he ob-served, "neighbors watch for trouble and offer aid and en-couragement to families. Children are expected to take direction respectfully from all adults. Relations between par-ents and offspring, and between husbands and wives, are sub-ject to informal social regulation. If mistreatment or neglect occurs, ostracism and sanctions will come from the whole community." From such a standpoint, it takes a grid-style block to raise a child.

Shame Encourages Censorship

Of course, cultural conservatives usually balk about what to do about those pesky nonjoiners, but sometimes, among os-tensibly friendly company, they let their guard down. I can recall a ghastly conversation I had in the early 1990s with a fellow Heritage Foundation policy analyst (who shall remain anonymous) on the subject of MTV. The network was a menace to the American family, he averred, but he noted a new technology (the V-chip) could enable parents to shield their children. I suggested in return that not all parents would be interested in such a contraption, and in fact some might even enjoy MTV. Chuckling and nodding his head, he responded: "We'll find out who these people are, and deal with them accordingly." He was not clear as to what he meant by "deal." I asked him if old-fashioned censorship would work. "I suppose it's too late for that," he answered. Too late! The implication was clear. If only we'd nipped Lenny Bruce, Hugh Hefner, William Burroughs, and Bob Dylan in the bud, the counterculture never would have grown out of control.

This leads to the second fatal design flaw of the campaign for moral censorship. Cultural conservatives would have people believe that shame merely substitutes for official cen-sorship. They don't want to be faced with the messy possi-bility that it leads to, and reinforces, censorship. Try this quick exercise: Ask a "nice" cultural conservative what he or she would do if moral censorship fails to achieve its purpose. Shame, after all, only can transform people with the capac-ity and willingness to feel it. The typical, nervous response will be something on the order of, "Well, maybe some government censorship would work, though I wouldn't want to overdo it." It never occurs to such people that honest artists and intellectuals resent "some" censorship, and just might fight back to prevent more to come. Bassist Krist Novoselic, who played for the band Nirvana and is an active lobbyist against censorship, is not the only person to observe that the mind of the censor starts at the "weird" edges of creativity, and gradually works its way toward the center.

In a perverse way, we owe a debt of gratitude to such paladins of the radical right as the American Enterprise Institute's Robert Bork and Irving Kristol. They freely admit official censorship must accompany the moral kind. The eighth chapter of Bork's most recent book, *Slouching Towards Gomorrah*, is titled "The Case for Censorship"—as in government censorship. Obsessed with rooting out "filth" from everyday life, he acknowledges the "tactical necessity" of shamership a la Bob Dole and Bill Bennett, but then makes clear the unpleasant duty ahead. "Is censorship really as unthinkable as we all seem to assume?" he asks. "That it is unthinkable is a very recent conceit. From the earliest colonies on this continent over 300 years ago, and for about 175 years of our existence as a nation, we endorsed and lived with censorship." For good measure, Bork adds, "By now we should have gotten over the liberal notion that its citizens' characters are none of the business of government." Meanwhile, Bork's AEI colleague, Irving Kristol (the husband of Gertrude Himmelfarb), weighs in with this blast at the film industry: "Censorship, some will say, is immoral—though no moral code of any society that has yet existed has ever deemed it so. And it is authoritarian. . . . (G)overnment, at various levels, will have to step in to help the parents. The difficult question is just how to intervene.". . .

There has always been—and always will be—disagreement about the limits of free expression and thought. But whatever one's views on these matters, the point is that censorship through shaming isn't so different from the legal kind; it should be viewed with similar skepticism, and combated with similar zeal. Let us be frank here: Prominent figures in culture, commerce, and politics are going to have to play hardball with censorship-minded conservatives. To their credit, some cyberspace leaders are not taking the moral thuggery lightly. "We're not going to censor down to the lowest common denominator. We let people make choices," says America Online's CEO and president Steve Case. He knows that moral censors don't like people to have choices, which is why they practically ran over each other to support the Communications Decency Act, which a panel of federal judges had the abundant good sense to block from taking effect ([in] December [1996] the Supreme Court agreed to review the case). Too bad the television industry didn't show more courage in resisting the spate of calls for tough, "voluntary" program ratings.

What is the likely result of this moral-legal crusade? What sort of bridge is it building for America's twenty-first century? A few strong hints can be gleaned from authoritarian paradises like Indonesia, Chile, and Singapore. Prosperity and fear coexist in those places—and conservatives like it that way. If none have artists and intellectuals of real significance (at least who can show their faces in public), families are protected. That's what really counts, right? Singapore has held out special promise for American virtuecrats, ever since it followed through on its promise to administer a brutal caning to a young American petty vandal, lending vivid meaning to the phrase, "This will hurt." Cal Thomas and Pat Buchanan, among other prominent conservatives, endorsed the punishment as the lad's just desserts. Thomas a few years earlier had praised Singapore's ban on the importation of Guns 'N Roses's *Use Your Illusion* double-CD release. That kind of tough talk may not exactly be fascism, but in America it's a fair imitation.

"Even though the law cannot compel us to make good choices, it can help us, at least indirectly, to change and grow morally."

The Government Should Legislate Morality

David A. Pendleton

In the viewpoint that follows, David A. Pendleton claims that it is essential for the government to intervene in matters of morality. The government has a duty to prohibit behavior that may cause harm to others, he claims. Pendleton is a member of the House of Representatives of the State of Hawaii.

As you read, consider the following questions:
1. What examples does the author provide of laws that "legislate morality"?
2. Why is making moral judgments unavoidable for government, in Pendleton's opinion?
3. When does behavior not qualify as private, as explained by the author?

Excerpted from "Good Laws and the Good Society," by David Pendleton, *America*, February 21, 1998. Reprinted with permission from the author.

I magine it is 35 years ago. You're outraged by the exclusion of African Americans by hotels, retail establishments and lunch counters. As part of a group discussing racial justice issues, you suggest that legislation banning discrimination in public accommodations and in interstate commerce might be in order. A defender of the status quo has a quick, sharp response: "No way! You cannot legislate morality."

He's not the only one who thinks that. Some liberals complain that opponents of abortion are "just trying to legislate morality." There are libertarians who say the same thing about people who want to regulate pornography and drug use. Some conservatives reject all attempts to legislate matters of economic behavior on the same basis. Across the political spectrum, lots of people seem to agree: You cannot legislate morality.

Why not? The law cannot force people to make good choices. It can, however, encourage people to develop new ways of thinking, seeing and feeling. Habits and practices we initially adopt to conform to authority can start to make sense to us over time. Sometimes it may take the pressure of an external demand to force us to see the value in a choice or a way of life we might otherwise dismiss. So, even though the law cannot compel us to make good choices, it can help us, at least indirectly, to change and grow morally. Someone who says it is impossible to legislate morality may be technically correct, but the law can certainly make a morally important difference in people's lives.

But maybe the objection to legislating morality is that there is so much moral disagreement in our society that no consensus can be reached and that we might be imposing moral convictions on people who do not accept them.

The fact is, though, that we do this all the time. Some people may believe that it is morally appropriate to kill those who belong to rival crime families. The law says it is not. Some people believe that it is morally appropriate to employ people in sweatshops under slave-like conditions. The law says it is not. Some people believe it is morally acceptable to cheat on their taxes. The law says it is not.

We cannot avoid making judgments—moral judgments—about what is true and false, about what is appropriate and inappropriate, what is acceptable in this country and what is not. Every time we determine what constitutes criminal behavior and what does not, how we will treat Native Hawaiians, how we will treat Filipino veterans, the quality of education we will provide our public school students, what safety net we will provide for the poor, what tax policies we will adopt, what military strategies we will follow—every time we make such a policy decision we are making moral judgments. That we disagree about issues of fundamental importance does not absolve us from deciding what we have to do and what we cannot do morally. Making moral judgments is a forced option for societies, just as it is for persons.

A person who agreed with what I have just argued might still respond by saying that, while of course we cannot avoid embodying some moral judgments in legislation, we should only be concerned with "public" morality. Such an objector might maintain that the basic purpose of an ordered society like ours is to enable people to pursue their individual goals without interference. As long as the government makes sure that people can cooperate effectively when they want to, the state has fulfilled its responsibilities. Of course, its legislation will presuppose some moral judgments, but not many.

There are several difficulties with this view. First, it is hard to have a society at all when the things people have in common are too few. Shared convictions and commitments are important if people are to experience real community life and if they are to join effectively and successfully in common endeavors.

Second, the objection only delivers the conclusion the objector wants if we agree to accept a very limited definition of what counts as a harm. Why should we? Victims of discrimination will surely be able to argue effectively that being treated as second-class citizens harms them. Pro-life advocates certainly have a case to make that abortion kills unborn human beings, just as pro-choice advocates can argue that abortion restrictions limit the choices of women. My point is not to settle any of the difficult moral arguments about these issues. I just want to maintain that we have no business ruling these kinds of discussion out of bounds in principle just because they do not conform to a narrow definition of what our government ought to be concerned with.

The Government Has a Duty to Protect Its Citizens

It is hard, in fact, to think of behavior that qualifies as private when that behavior harms someone else—someone whom the government has a duty to protect. Everything we do affects other people directly or indirectly. So other people have good reason to be interested in how I live my life.

Tabloid journalists have capitalized in vicious ways on the pain of others; we do not need to know the details of our politicians' sex lives. But we have every reason to be concerned with the character and integrity of those who lead us, who direct our sons and daughters in battle, who determine how our tax dollars ought to be spent: their closely held values will determine how they function in our government. In the same way, each of us has some reason to be concerned with the behavior of others. If we are to live together as neighbors, friends, Americans, what we do will unavoidably affect those with whom we share our lives, for good or for ill. We cannot, therefore, demand that they ignore things we do that are hurtful or harmful to them or to others because our actions are "private."

"Oh, great! Just what we need . . . religious fanatics!"

The days are long gone when an abusive husband or father could claim that legal authorities had no right to challenge his actions because they occurred within the private sanctuary of his home. But we continue to act as if the harm some people do can be ignored because confronting them might require us to legislate private morality. I think the civil rights example should make us suspicious of doing so. I firmly believe that it is important to avoid bureaucratic intrusions, invasive confrontations, a return to Prohibition or the birth of a police state. I am saying that if we want to live well together, we have to make choices about the kind of community we want to be and the kinds of persons we want to be.

That will mean tackling tough issues. It will almost always mean making moral judgments. Necessarily, then, it will mean legislating morality. That's not something we need to find embarrassing. It simply means being deliberate and judicious, courageous yet prudent, as we carefully craft policies that will address all the threats that face us and our families, as we try to construct a better society for our children who inherit the world we leave behind.

"The power of the government should never be used except to protect public health and public safety."

The Government Should Not Legislate Morality

Charley Reese

In the subsequent viewpoint, nationally syndicated columnist Charley Reese asserts that the government has no business solving America's moral problems. He claims that the government has neither the right nor the ability to intervene in moral issues. In Reese's view, if America is to become a better society, individuals must take responsibility for their actions and stop engaging in immoral behavior.

As you read, consider the following questions:

1. What evidence does Reese provide that people in America have "gone sour"?
2. What is the appropriate role of government, as stated by Reese?
3. According to the author, what is the danger in asking the government to solve problems of morality?

Excerpted from "Congress Can't Restore the Family," by Charley Reese, *Conservative Chronicle*, August 19, 1998. Reprinted with the permission of King Features Syndicate.

I noticed in a directory of conservative organizations a proliferation of organizations concerned about the family. Most of them claim to have an interest in "public policy" matters.

Sorry, folks. The imperial government is guilty of a lot of stuff, but it is as innocent as Snow White on this issue. The government did not break the American family. The government cannot restore the American family.

A Morality Issue, Not a Public Policy Issue

When you hear a politician claiming to be interested in "restoring" the family, write him off as a demagogue or a fool. No law, no appropriation, no bureaucratic program can fix what's wrong. It's all personal and private. It's a morality issue, not a public policy issue. It's not just the government that has gone sour in America: it's the people.

It's people who spend $8 billion a year on pornography. It's people who spend God knows how many billions in gambling casinos. It's people who take vows and break them. It's the people who bring children into the world and abort, abandon or abuse them. It's people who watch Jerry Springer or listen to Howard Stern. It's the people who patronize trash. It's people who approve of Bill Clinton, a sleaze and failed president.

The government has nothing to do with it. The government didn't corrupt anybody. It would be closer to the mark to say people have corrupted the government.

The first idea Americans ought to get over is that government can fix whatever we decide ails us at any given moment. Government is quite limited in what it can do. It is just force. The government can kill people, confiscate their property, deprive them of liberty or threaten them with all of the above. It can confiscate money and write checks on the confiscated money and thus buy votes. That's it as far as basic powers go.

Wise citizens would be as leery of asking the government to solve a problem as they would be of asking a wolf to watch their children. The problem won't get solved, but the government will use the attempt as an excuse to widen its jurisdiction into even more areas of our lives—and, naturally, confiscate even more of our money.

Traditional Americans believed, and wisely so, that the power of government should never be used except to protect public health and public safety. It should act only to protect people from communicable diseases, force and fraud. If we could ever re-chain the federal government to the Constitution, it could easily live off revenue tariffs and the proceeds of the sale of public land.

The Role of Personal Responsibility

The second idea Americans ought to get shut of is that if they do something wrong, it's somebody else's fault. Everyone has heard of a free market in goods and services. Well, the free market of morality is even freer.

Mark Thornhill, *North (San Diego) County Times.*

People can choose their own character. All it takes to be a truthful person is a decision not to tell lies. All it takes to be brave is the decision to do what has to be done despite one's fears. Whatever we choose to be, in terms of character, we are free to be. No one can make us lie, cheat, steal, rob, murder or abandon people we are responsible for. When these things happen, it's because people freely choose to do them.

Teaching morality is the province of parents and religion. If they fail, the government can't do it instead. George Washington's argument is still valid. He said republican government depends on a virtuous people. No means of instilling virtue has been found to be superior to religion. Therefore, he said, anyone who is an enemy of religion is an enemy of republican government.

A government cannot make bad people good, but good people can make bad government good.

| *"Character education is one of the most, if not the most, important answer to our national crisis of character."*

Public Schools Should Provide Character Education

Sanford N. McDonnell

Sanford N. McDonnell is chairman of the Character Education Partnership, a national coalition of organizations and individuals working to implement a public school curriculum that teaches ethical values. In the following viewpoint, McDonnell contends that such a curriculum would teach young people the importance of honesty, responsibility, respect, and hard work. The character education programs already in existence have improved student behavior, he maintains, as well as academic performance.

Editor's note: This article, which originally appeared in the Wall Street Journal, *was signed by more than two dozen of the Character Education Partnership's advisory board, including Barbara Bush and Jesse Jackson.*

As you read, consider the following questions:

1. According to McDonnell, what is the answer to overcoming today's national crisis of character?
2. What impact did character education have on Allen Elementary School and Jefferson Junior High School, as stated by the author?
3. What does the author list as the ten basic principles of character education?

Throughout most of our history, certain core ethical values were considered fundamental to the character of the nation and to the character of the people who made up the nation. These values were passed on from generation to generation in the home, the school and the church.

Today in America, far too many homes, schools and churches are no longer fulfilling their traditional roles as protectors and promoters of ethical values. Too many young people are growing up with almost no exposure to the values upon which our freedom is based. To paraphrase Newt Gingrich, today we have 12-year-olds selling drugs, 14-year-olds having babies, 16-year-olds killing each other, and kids of all ages admitting to lying, cheating and stealing at record numbers. The answer is a return to the core values of our American heritage in our homes, schools, businesses, government, and indeed in each of our daily lives. But it is the schools that have the greatest potential for overcoming this national crisis of character.

During most of our history, character education was considered just as important as intellectual knowledge. During the past 30 years or more, for various reasons, formal character education was largely removed from the public schools; but in response to our national crisis of character, many school communities across the country have been reinstating character education. They are realizing that while they can't teach religion in the public schools anymore, they can teach the core values common to all the great religions.

Over the past decade, character education has been successfully implemented in public schools, kindergarten through high school, in many parts of the nation. And where it has been implemented properly, it has produced positive and often dramatic results not only in student behavior but also in academic performance.

The Allen Elementary School, an inner-city school in Dayton, Ohio, with 60% of its students coming from single-parent homes and 70% from families on welfare, was a near disaster in 1989. Allen was ranked 28th out of Dayton's 33 elementary schools in test scores, and teachers couldn't teach because of the constant discipline problems. Principal Rudy Bernardo implemented a comprehensive character education program; five years later Allen was No. 1 in test scores and its behavior problems had improved dramatically.

Jefferson Junior High School, an inner-city school in Washington, D.C., with approximately 800 African-American students, was having serious problems with drugs, student pregnancies and discipline. With a comprehensive character education program, Principal Vera White completely turned the school around over a five-year period. There have been almost no student pregnancies in the past few years, and Jefferson has been recognized for having the highest academic achievement in the city. The school now has a waiting list of more than 400 students.

The nonprofit Character Education Partnership, a growing national coalition of organizations and individuals, was founded in February 1993 to help communities across the nation implement character education in their public schools. CEP defines "good character" as understanding, caring about and acting on core ethical values. CEP believes that character education is most effectively accomplished using the following 10 basic principles:

First and foremost, the entire school faculty and staff must be ethical role models.

Second, core values such as honesty, responsibility, respect and hard work must be promoted in all phases of school life.

Third, the school must become a caring community, progressing toward becoming a microcosm of the civil, caring and just society we seek to be as a nation.

Fourth, students must have many and varied opportunities to apply values such as responsibility and fairness in everyday interactions in and out of the classroom.

Fifth, effective character education includes high academic standards that challenge all students to set high goals, work hard to achieve them and persevere in the face of difficulty.

Sixth, teachers should teach core values through subjects such as language arts, science and social studies; and engage students in moral reflection through reading, writing and discussion.

Seventh, teachers should practice moral discipline using the creation and enforcement of rules as opportunities to foster moral reasoning and respect for others.

Eighth, character education as well as academic progress must be evaluated in every school. As the old Navy saying goes, "You can expect what you inspect." The character of the school, each aspect of its character education, and the extent to which students manifest good character should all be assessed.

Ninth, the principal and his or her entire staff should use the total school environment to support and amplify the values taught in the classroom. For example, service opportunities in the school and in the community help students learn to care by giving care.

The Challenge of Character Education

As societal moral problems continue to worsen, schools and communities across the country are joining an effort to build a better society and better schools by building the character of our children. . . .

The premise of the character-education movement is straightforward. Irresponsible and destructive behaviors such as violence, dishonesty, drug abuse, sexual promiscuity, and a poor work ethic have a common core: the absence of good character. Educating for good character, unlike piecemeal reforms, offers the promise of improvement in all these areas. The challenge the movement sets before the nation is all-encompassing: for families, schools, faith communities, youth organizations, business, government, and the media—all those who touch the lives of the young—to come together in common cause to elevate the character of our youth and, ultimately, of society as a whole.

Thomas Lickona, *World & I*, June 1, 1996.

Tenth, parents, churches, businesses, and indeed the total adult community should be recruited as full partners in character building.

Character education is one of the most, if not *the* most, important answer to our national crisis of character. We need to implement character education as fast as possible in every school in America as part of any truly effective education reform movement.

Character without knowledge is weak and feeble, but

knowledge without character is dangerous and a potential menace to society. America will not be strong if we graduate young people from our schools who are brilliant but dishonest, who have great intellectual knowledge but don't care about others, who are highly creative thinkers but are irresponsible. Martin Luther King Jr. stated it well: "Intelligence plus character—that is the goal of true education."

> *"Ethics is best left to families, religious institutions and private schools. Public education will only muck things up."*

Public Schools Should Not Provide Character Education

Don Feder

In the subsequent viewpoint, Don Feder explains why he believes character education—programs that attempt to teach ethical values in the public schools—will inevitably fail. In Feder's view, character education takes on the impossible task of teaching morality without mentioning religion. In addition, he argues, public educators may impart dangerous values to children. Feder is a nationally syndicated columnist.

As you read, consider the following questions:
1. Why is it difficult to keep religion out of a discussion of morality, in Feder's opinion?
2. According to the author, what is the time-honored fashion of instilling moral behavior in children, and why is this method superior to character education?
3. Why does Feder fear public educators imparting their values to children?

Reprinted from "Schools Will Muck Up Character Education," by Don Feder, *Conservative Chronicle*, June 16, 1999. Reprinted with the permission of Don Feder and Creators Syndicate.

Despite the abject failure of public schools at teaching academic subjects, there's no shortage of proposals to get them into other areas of learning where they'll probably be even less successful—if we're lucky.

Now cometh character education, whose advent was heralded in the *New York Times* in June 1999. Its vanguard is a group called The Character Education Partnership.

The recent spate of school shootings and Supreme Court ruling on sexual harassment has turned our thoughts to how nice it would be to have schools where kids didn't use each other for target practice and adolescent boys didn't act like Bill Clinton around adolescent girls.

Since the '60s, when the Supreme Court determined that God was trespassing when His name was invoked in the classroom, schools have become value-neutral zones. But now, oh happy day, there's a rising tide of secular character pedagogy.

The Character Education Partnership

The Partnership is a coalition including teachers' unions, National PTA and other usual suspects. To guide educators, it's developed Eleven Principles of Effective Character Education. First, "decide on universal values—such as caring, honesty, fairness, responsibility and respect for others." (Aren't universal values self-evident? If so, why did they have to be decided on?)

Then, get students talking about these values, studying real-life examples and practicing them, the Partnership urges.

Trying to keep religion out of a discussion of morality complicates matters. The principal of a San Diego elementary school explained that, in naming its character curriculum, "virtues" and "values" were rejected for their religious overtones. Instead, the program is called (yawn) "interactive skills." You returned lost property to its rightful owner? Great interactive skills!

Liberals are forever trying to teach virtue without faith, which is akin to instructing a blind man in landscape painting.

Point seven in the Partnership's principles claims character education "needs to ensure that positive character development grows out of a student's *intrinsic* motivation to 'know the good, love the good and do the good,' rather than extrinsic consequences, such as rewards and punishment."

But there is no intrinsic motivation to know the good, just as there are no innate values.

Teacher Objections to Character Education

In some cases . . . teachers view the new demands as clashing with their constitutional rights.

• In Collinsville, Ill., the teachers' union is protesting a new policy on obscene language that calls on teachers to serve as "positive role models" and "ambassadors for the school district." The union chafes at the "vague" policy especially because it's not clear if it applies after school hours.

• In Santa Ana, California, teachers balk at having to wear suits and dresses after a tough dress code is put in place for students.

• Last month, a gay teacher in Salt Lake City sued the school district after it removed her from coaching volleyball and told her not to talk about her "lifestyle."

• In Florida, an unmarried teacher is reassigned after becoming pregnant.

Laurel Shaper Walters, *Christian Science Monitor*, November 5, 1997.

What happens when values conflict? Honesty and loyalty are both positive traits. If your friend steals, do you lie to protect him or break faith by telling the truth? Character education, which can't prioritize, has no answer and says, in effect, you decide.

Religion and Morality

For generations, proper behavior was instilled in students in time-honored fashion. There were prayers and *Bible* readings. In the previous century, *McGuffey's Readers* taught morality along with literacy.

This was reinforced by extrinsic consequences: If you're odious, teacher will hit you with her ruler. If you're angelic, you may just get into Heaven.

Caring, honesty, responsibility and respect for others are universal because they were ordained by the Master of the Universe.

Throughout the course of history, more often than not, societies practiced far different values—as wars of conquest, slavery, extermination, oppression and the opulence of ruling classes, borne by the misery of the masses, attest.

It's one thing to tell kids: "Here are a set of universal values. Practice them because bad things happen when they're widely ignored." (Presidents begin having sex with interns, lying to the American people, committing perjury and bombing civilian populations.)

It's quite another to promote adherence to rules of ethical behavior by noting that they emanate from the source of life. You might call them an operating manual for humanity.

When asked by one of the Littleton gunmen if she believed in God, Cassie Bernall said yes, knowing the consequences. Such integrity in the face of certain death isn't instilled by instruction in "interactive skills."

Finally, do we want public educators imparting their values?

Consider the job they've done with sex education, their assault on modesty. Do you want a card-carrying member of the National Education Association—which thinks abortion is a right and two men are a family—teaching your children right from wrong?

Public schools should insist on certain minimal standards (don't snap Susie's bra, don't give Willie a wedgie because he's a nerd, don't cheat on exams), reinforced by strict discipline. Ethics is best left to families, religious institutions and private schools. Public education will only muck things up.

Periodical Bibliography

The following articles have been selected to supplement the diverse views presented in this chapter. Addresses are provided for periodicals not indexed in the *Readers' Guide to Periodical Literature*, the *Alternative Press Index*, the *Social Sciences Index*, or the *Index to Legal Periodicals and Books*.

Gary Bauer	"The Most Crucial Issues," *World & I*, March 1, 1997. Available from 3400 New York Ave. NE, Washington, DC 20002.
Linda Bowles	"Shameless Culture Provides Dangerous Solutions," *Conservative Chronicle*, December 16, 1998. Available from PO Box 37077, Boone, IA 50037-0077.
Ethan Bronner	"Teaching Values Without Taking a Page from the Bible," *New York Times*, June 1, 1999.
Hillary Rodham Clinton	"Civil Society: The Space That Matters Most," *New Perspectives Quarterly*, Spring 1998.
Michael Clough	"Civil Society and the Future of the Nation-State," *Nation*, February 22, 1999.
Don E. Eberly	"Renewing American Culture," *American Outlook*, Winter 1999. Available from PO Box 26-919, Indianapolis, IN 46226.
Jean Bethke Elshtain	"A Call to Civil Society," *Society*, July/August 1999.
Nick Gillespie	"Truth Squad: The Coercive Agenda Behind the 'Civil Society' Movement," *Reason*, August/September 1998.
Stephen Goode	"We Love You, Nanny Dearest," *Insight*, July 27, 1998. Available from 3600 New York Ave. NE, Washington, DC 20002.
David Hartman	"Restoring Families by Restricting Government," *Chronicles*, May 1999. Available from 928 N. Main St., Rockford, IL 61103.
Donald Lambro	"Don't Look to Washington for Moral Leadership," *Conservative Chronicle*, July 29, 1998.
Robert Rector	"God and the Underclass," *National Review*, July 15, 1996.

For Further Discussion

Chapter 1

1. Theodore Forstmann argues that capitalism promotes freedom of choice and rewards individual achievement. David Hilfiker, on the other hand, contends that capitalism fosters selfishness and greed, and undermines the dignity of work. Whose argument is more persuasive, and why? Based on what you have read in these viewpoints, does capitalism's philosophy benefit American society? Why or why not?

2. Philip Yancey maintains that without the guidance of religion, society has no way of distinguishing between right and wrong. Do you agree with his belief that religion is the only reliable guide to determining what is right and wrong? What alternative view does Dave Matson propose?

3. According to Jean Bethke Elshtain, the breakdown of the traditional, two-parent family is the cause of a variety of social problems, including poverty, crime, illegitimacy, and drug abuse. How do Arlene Skolnick and Stacey Rosencrantz refute this claim? In your opinion, what type of family is most likely to raise happy children?

Chapter 2

1. William J. Bennett argues that society is experiencing moral decline. James A. Morone disagrees. What facts and statistics do Bennett and Morone provide to support their cases? Is their evidence contradictory? Whose evidence do you find more persuasive, and why?

2. Describe popular culture as Herbert I. London characterizes it, and as Tyler Cowen characterizes it. Which description is more accurate, and why? Is there more reason to be negative or positive about the state of popular culture in America? Explain your answer.

3. Do you agree with David Klepper and James B. Twitchell that America is a materialistic society? Why or why not? In what ways does consumerism harm society, in Klepper's opinion? How does Twitchell refute the claim that consumerism is entirely negative?

4. Based on what you have read in this chapter, do you feel that America is in moral decline? Provide specific examples to support your answer.

Chapter 3

1. For what reasons does Gregg Easterbrook believe that media violence harms society? How does Danny Goldberg address these claims? Who makes a stronger case, and why?

2. Based on what you have read in this chapter, do you feel that the media's influence on society is generally positive or generally negative? Why or why not? Give specific examples to support your claim.

Chapter 4

1. Based on what you have read by James B. Twitchell and Carl F. Horowitz, is shame a feasible approach to improving America's values? Why or why not? List the possible consequences of societal shame, as stated by Twitchell and Horowitz.

2. How do David A. Pendleton and Charley Reese differ in their views on whether the government should be involved in issues of morality? Which perspective do you find more convincing, and why? Does the U.S. government currently prohibit certain behaviors solely on the basis of morality? List the examples cited in the viewpoints, or any others you can think of.

3. What is character education, as described by Sanford N. McDonnell? What are Don Feder's objections to character education? Do you agree with Feder's view that parents and religion are better suited to teach values than character education programs? Why or why not?

Organizations to Contact

The editors have compiled the following list of organizations concerned with the issues debated in this book. The descriptions are derived from materials provided by the organizations. All have publications or information available for interested readers. The list was compiled on the date of publication of the present volume; the information provided here may change. Be aware that many organizations take several weeks or longer to respond to inquiries, so allow as much time as possible.

American Alliance for Rights and Responsibilities (AARR)
1725 K St. NW, Suite 1112, Washington, DC 20006
(202) 785-7844 • fax: (202) 785-4370

AARR believes that democracy can work only if the defense of individual rights is matched by a commitment to individual and social responsibility. It is dedicated to restoring the balance between rights and responsibilities in American life. It publishes the bimonthly newsletter *Rights and Responsibilities*.

American Atheists
PO Box 5733, Parsippany, NJ 07054-6733
(908) 276-7300 • fax: (908) 276-7402
e-mail: info@atheists.org • website: http://www.atheists.org

American Atheists is an educational organization dedicated to the complete and absolute separation of church and state. It opposes religious involvement such as prayer and religious clubs in public schools. The organization's purpose is to stimulate freedom of thought and inquiry concerning religious beliefs and practices. It publishes the monthly *American Atheist Newsletter*.

American Civil Liberties Union (ACLU)
125 Broad St., 18th Floor, New York, NY 10004
(212) 549-2500 • fax: (212) 549-2646
website: http://www.aclu.org

The ACLU is a national organization that works to defend Americans' civil rights as guaranteed by the U.S. Constitution. It works to establish equality before the law, regardless of race, color, sexual orientation, or national origin. The ACLU publishes and distributes policy statements, pamphlets, and the semiannual newsletter *Civil Liberties Alert*.

Cato Institute
1000 Massachusetts Ave. NW, Washington, DC 20001-5403
(202) 842-0200 • fax: (202) 842-3490
e-mail: cato@cato.org • website: http://www.cato.org
The Cato Institute is a libertarian public policy research foundation dedicated to limiting the control of government and protecting individual liberties. It offers numerous publications on public policy issues, including the triennial *Cato Journal*, the bimonthly newsletter *Cato Policy Report*, and the quarterly magazine *Regulation*.

Center for Media and Public Affairs (CMPA)
2101 L St. NW, Suite 405, Washington, DC 20037
(202) 223-2942 • fax: (202) 872-4014
e-mail: cmpamm@aol.com • website: http://www.cmpa.com
CMPA is a research organization that studies the media treatment of social and political affairs. It uses surveys to measure the media's influence on public opinion. It publishes the monthly *Media Monitor*, the monograph *A Day of Television Violence*, and various other books, articles, and monographs.

Center for Media Literacy
4727 Wilshire Blvd., Suite 403, Los Angeles, CA 90010
(323) 931-4177 • fax: (323) 931-4474
e-mail: cml@medialit.org • website: http://www.medialit.org
The center is a media education organization. It seeks to give the public power over the media by fostering media literacy. It publishes the quarterly *Media & Values*.

Christian Coalition (CC)
1801-L Sara Dr., Chesapeake, VA 23320
(804) 424-2630 • fax: (804) 434-9068
e-mail: coalition@cc.org • website: http://www.cc.org
Founded by evangelist Pat Robertson, the coalition is a grassroots political organization of Christian fundamentalists working to stop what it believes is the moral decay of government. The coalition seeks to elect moral legislators and opposes extramarital sex and comprehensive drug and sex education. Its publications include the monthly newsletter *The Religious Right Watch* and the monthly tabloid *Christian American*.

Eagle Forum
PO Box 618, Alton, IL 62002
(618) 462-5415 • fax: (618) 462-8909
e-mail: eagle@eagleforum.org
website: http://www.eagleforum.org

Eagle Forum is a Christian group that promotes morality and traditional family values as revealed through the Bible. It opposes many facets of public education and liberal government. The forum publishes the monthly *Phyllis Schlafly Report* and a periodic newsletter.

Family Research Council (FRC)
801 G St. NW, Washington, DC 20001
(202) 393-2100 • fax: (202) 393-2134
e-mail: corrdept@frc.org • website: http://www.frc.org

The council is a research, resource, and education organization that promotes the traditional family, which it defines as a group of people bound by marriage, blood, or adoption. It opposes schools' tolerance of homosexuality and school condom distribution programs. The council publishes numerous reports from a conservative perspective. These publications include the monthly newsletter *Washington Watch*, the bimonthly journal *Family Policy*, and *Free to Be Family*, a report that focuses on children and families.

The Heritage Foundation
214 Massachusetts Ave. NE, Washington, DC 20002-4999
(202) 546-4400 • (800) 544-4843 • fax: (202) 544-6979
e-mail: pubs@heritage.org • website: http://www.heritage.org

The Heritage Foundation is a conservative public policy research institute that advocates free-market economics and limited government. Its publications include the monthly *Policy Review*, the Backgrounder series of occasional papers, and the Heritage Lectures series.

Josephson Institute of Ethics
4640 Admiralty Way, Suite 1001, Marina del Rey, CA 90292
(310) 306-1868 • fax: (310) 827-1864
e-mail: ji-pub@primenet.com
website: http://www.josephsoninstitute.org

The institute is a nonprofit membership organization founded to improve the ethical quality of society by teaching and advocating principled reasoning and ethical decisionmaking. Its Government Ethics Center has conducted programs and workshops for more than twenty thousand influential leaders. Its publications include the periodic newsletter *Ethics in Action*, the quarterly *Ethics: Easier Said Than Done*, and reports such as *Ethics of American Youth: A Warning and a Call to Action*.

Morality in Media (MIM)
475 Riverside Dr., Suite 239, New York, NY 10115
(212) 870-3222 • fax: (212) 870-2765
e-mail: mim@moralityinmedia.org
website: http://www.moralityinmedia.org

MIM opposes what it considers to be indecency in broadcasting—especially the broadcasting of pornography. It works to educate and organize the public in support of strict decency laws, and it has launched an annual "turn off TV day" to protest offensive television programming. The group publishes the *Morality in Media Newsletter* and the handbook *TV: The World's Greatest Mind-Bender*.

National Coalition Against Censorship (NCAC)
275 7th Ave., New York, NY 10001
(212) 807-6222 • fax: (212) 807-6245
e-mail: ncac@ncac.org • website: http://www.ncac.org

NCAC is an alliance of organizations committed to defending freedom of thought, inquiry, and expression by engaging in public education and advocacy on national and local levels. It publishes periodic reports and the monthly *Censorship News*.

National Organization for Women (NOW)
1000 16th St. NW, Suite 700, Washington, DC 20036
(202) 331-0066 • fax: (202) 785-8576
e-mail: now@now.org • website: http://www.now.org

NOW is one of the largest and most influential feminist organizations in the United States. It seeks to end prejudice and discrimination against women in all areas of life. It lobbies legislatures for more equitable laws and works to educate and inform the public on women's issues. NOW publishes the bimonthly tabloid *NOW Times*, policy statements, and articles.

Parents, Families, and Friends of Lesbians and Gays (PFLAG)
1101 14th St., NW Suite 1030, Washington, DC 20005
(202) 638-4200 • fax: (202) 638-0243
e-mail: info@pflag.org • website: http://www.pflag.org

PFLAG is an international organization that provides support, education, and advocacy services for gays, lesbians, bisexuals, and their families and friends. It works to end prejudice and discrimination against gays, lesbians, and bisexuals. It publishes and distributes the pamphlets *About Our Children*, *Coming Out to Your Parents*, and *Why is My Child Gay?*

People for the American Way (PFAW)
2000 M St. NW, Suite 400, Washington, DC 20036
(202) 467-4999 • fax: (202) 293-2672
e-mail: pfaw@pfaw.org • website: http://www.pfaw.org

PFAW works to increase tolerance and respect for America's diverse cultures, religions, and values such as freedom of expression. It distributes educational materials, leaflets, and brochures and publishes the quarterly *Press Clips*, a collection of newspaper articles concerning censorship.

Progressive Policy Institute (PPI)
600 Pennsylvania Ave. SE, Suite 400, Washington, DC 20003
(202) 546-0007 • fax: (202) 544-5014
website: http://www.dlcppi.org

PPI is a public policy research organization that strives to develop alternatives to the traditional debate between liberals and conservatives. It advocates economic policies designed to stimulate broad upward mobility and social policies designed to liberate the poor from poverty and dependence. The institute publishes the book *Building the Bridge: 10 Big Ideas to Transform America*.

Single Parent Resource Center (SPRC)
141 W. 28th St., Suite 302, New York, NY 10001
(212) 947-0221
website: http://singleparentresources.com

The center is a clearinghouse for information about and for single parents. It maintains that as a growing number of children are raised in single-parent families, more aid will be needed to help single parents make good decisions for themselves and their children. SPRC publishes pamphlets on single-parent issues.

Bibliography of Books

William J. Bennett — *The Death of Outrage: Bill Clinton and the Assault on American Ideals*. New York: Free Press, 1998.

Robert H. Bork — *Slouching Towards Gomorrah: Modern Liberalism and American Decline*. New York: ReganBooks, 1996.

Stephen L. Carter — *Civility: Manners, Morals, and the Etiquette of Democracy*. New York: BasicBooks, 1998.

Lynne V. Cheney — *Telling the Truth: Why Our Culture and Our Country Have Stopped Making Sense—and What We Can Do About It*. New York: Simon & Schuster, 1995.

Harry M. Clor — *Public Morality and Liberal Society: Essays on Decency, Law, and Pornography*. Notre Dame: University of Notre Dame Press, 1997.

Robert Coles — *The Moral Intelligence of Children: How to Raise a Moral Child*. New York: Random House, 1997.

Tyler Cowen — *In Praise of Commercial Culture*. Cambridge, MA: Harvard University Press, 1998.

Mark Dery — *The Pyrotechnic Insanitarium: American Culture on the Brink*. New York: Grove Press, 1999.

Dick DeVos — *Rediscovering American Values*. New York: Dutton, 1997.

B.K. Eakman — *Cloning of the American Mind: Eradicating Morality Through Education*. Lafayette, LA: Huntington House, 1998.

Thomas Frank — *The Conquest of Cool*. Chicago: University of Chicago Press, 1997.

Ellen G. Friedman and Corinne Squire — *Morality USA*. Minneapolis: University of Minnesota Press, 1998.

Francis Fukuyama — *The Great Disruption: Human Nature and the Reconstitution of Social Order*. New York: Free Press, 1999.

Richard T. Gill — *Posterity Lost: Progress, Ideology, and the Decline of the American Family*. Lanham, MD: Rowman & Littlefield, 1999.

Todd Gitlin — *The Twilight of Common Dreams: Why America Is Wracked by Culture Wars*. New York: Henry Holt, 1995.

Martin L. Gross — *The End of Sanity: Social and Cultural Madness in America*. New York: Avon Books, 1997.

John A. Hall and   *Is America Breaking Apart?* Princeton, NJ:
Charles Lindholm   Princeton University Press, 1999.

Sylvia Ann Hewlett   *The War Against Parents: What We Can Do for*
and Cornel West   *America's Beleaguered Moms and Dads.* Boston:
Houghton Mifflin, 1998.

Gertrude Himmelfarb   *The De-moralization of Society: From Victorian*
Virtues to Modern Values. New York: Knopf,
1995.

Jon Katz   *Virtuous Reality: How America Surrendered Dis-*
cussion of Moral Values to Opportunists, Nitwits &
Blockheads Like William Bennett. New York:
Random House, 1997.

Peter Kreeft   *Ecumenical Jihad: Ecumenism and the Culture*
War. San Francisco: Ignatius Press, 1996.

George Lakoff   *Moral Politics: What Conservatives Know That*
Liberals Don't. Chicago: University of Chicago
Press, 1996.

Michael Lerner   *The Politics of Meaning: Restoring Hope and*
Possibility in an Age of Cynicism. Reading, MA:
Addison-Wesley, 1996.

Dana Mack   *The Assault on Parenthood: How Our Culture Un-*
dermines the Family. New York: Simon & Schuster, 1997.

James A. Michener   *This Noble Land: My Vision for America.* New
York: Random House, 1996.

Nicolaus Mills   *The Triumph of Meanness: America's War Against*
Its Better Self. Boston: Houghton Mifflin, 1997.

Michael Parenti   *America Besieged.* San Francisco: City Lights
Books, 1998.

Michael Parenti   *Land of Idols: Political Mythology in America.* New
York: St. Martin's Press, 1994.

D.Z. Phillips   *Religion and Morality.* New York: St. Martin's
Press, 1996.

Dan Quayle and   *The American Family: Discovering the Values That*
and Diane Medved   *Make Us Strong.* New York: HarperCollins,
1996.

Matt Ridley   *The Origins of Virtue: Human Instincts and the*
Evolution of Cooperation. New York: Viking,
1997.

Juliet B. Schor   *The Overspent American: Upscaling, Downshifting,*
and the New Consumer. New York: BasicBooks,
1998.

Wendy Shalit   *A Return to Modesty: Discovering the Lost Virtue.*
New York: Free Press, 1999.

Judith Stacey

In the Name of the Family: Rethinking Family Values in the Postmodern Age. Boston: Beacon Press, 1996.

Cal Thomas

The Things That Matter Most. New York: Harper-Collins, 1994.

James B. Twitchell

For Shame: The Loss of Common Decency in American Culture. New York: St. Martin's Press, 1997.

James B. Twitchell

Lead Us Into Temptation: The Triumph of American Materialism. New York: Columbia University Press, 1999.

Samuel Walker

The Rights Revolution: Rights and Community in Modern America. New York: Oxford University Press, 1998.

Ben J. Wattenberg

Values Matter Most: How Republicans or Democrats or a Third Party Can Win and Renew the American Way of Life. New York: Free Press, 1995.

John K. Wilson

The Myth of Political Correctness. Durham, NC: Duke University Press, 1995.

Alan Wolfe

One Nation, After All: What Middle-Class Americans Really Think About God, Country, Family, Racism, Welfare, Immigration, Homosexuality, Work, the Right, the Left, and Each Other. New York: Viking, 1998.

Index